BECOMING
A MENTAL
MATH WIZARD

Jerry
Lucas

D0822456

SHOE TREE PRESS
WHITE HALL, VIRGINIA

Published by Shoe Tree Press
an imprint of Betterway Publications, Inc.
P.O. Box 219
Crozet, VA 22932
(804) 823-5661

Cover design by Rick Britton
Typography by East Coast Typography, Inc.

Library of Congress Cataloging-in-Publication Data

Lucas, Jerry, 1950—
    Becoming a mental math wizard / Jerry Lucas.
      p. cm.
    Includes index.
    Summary: An effort to make math fun through doing and performing rather than studying and pondering.
    ISBN 1-55870-216-4
    1. Mathematics—Juvenile literature. [1. Mathematics.]
I. Title.
QA40.5.L83   1991
372.7—dc20   91-19472
                                       CIP
                                       AC

Printed in the United States of America
0 9 8 7 6 5 4 3

ACKNOWLEDGMENTS

First I would like to thank the entire staff of Betterway Publications. I have truly enjoyed working with all of them to make this book a reality.

I would next like to thank Eugene Novagratsky, Jim Stein, James Wang, Ben Chen, Ming-Lung Lee, and Paul Seah for the many productive and thought-provoking technical discussions they have had with me.

I owe special thanks to George and Marianne Steinis and to Eugene Novagratsky, who each spent several hours of their own time as informal book reviewers. Joe Stein, age ten, served as a youthful reviewer for the material in Chapters 1, 2, 3, 4, and 15.

Sal Mazzurco, John Reilly, and Dave Plummer assisted with research in supplying data for problems.

Bruce Bell and Evelyn Nichols provided valuable thoughts on the book's layout, organization, and tone.

Special thanks are due to Sheryl Kelly for her excellent work in preparing the manuscript for publication.

Affectionate and loving thanks to my wife Kerry, whose unswerving enthusiasm and encouragement helped bring this book to completion.

Finally, a very special thanks to my parents, Mr. and Mrs. Gerard R. Lucas, currently of Williamsville, New York, who did so much to encourage my development in mathematics.

FIGURES

TABLES

EQUATIONS

Contents

Introduction

Is it possible to make math fun? It is a subject that requires an enormous amount of effort and discomfort. To many people it is drab and uninteresting. With all the distractions that modern society has to offer, it is difficult to imagine someone choosing to spend a few hours working on math problems. Yet there are people who do, and who enjoy it.

A curious parallel can be observed in the world of athletics. Many sports such as running, swimming, and gymnastics require enormous amounts of effort and commitment, and, for the most part, are not fun. Yet, we don't have to look long and hard to see thousands of people just like us swimming laps in a pool or running circles around a track. What is it that motivates these people?

At various times during my life I have been a competitive swimmer, a math student, a swimming coach, and a math teacher. I have come to believe that those who pursue athletics and those who pursue mathematics experience the same type of motivation. This motivation springs from the joy of improving yourself or accomplishing something that you formerly had thought of as an unlikely or impossible feat. The joy that the swimmer or runner feels upon doing his best time is essentially the same joy that the math student feels upon succeeding at a difficult problem. Once you have experienced this joy, you will work still harder to experience it again.

It is from this viewpoint that this book is written. The goal is to give readers a sense of joy at accomplishing feats of math that might at first seem impossible. Early on, readers are instructed and encouraged to attempt problems beyond their present abilities, and in fact beyond the abilities of most of the population. I believe the average reader will significantly advance his abilities without feeling unduly stressed or overworked.

The method used by Hippocrates to construct the quadrature of the lune, and the approximation of π developed by Sir Isaac Newton provide beautiful examples of mathematical genius. But you won't find them in this book. The idea of this book is not to sit quietly and admire the genius of famous mathematicians. The idea is to provide readers with the necessary skills and encouragement to solve their own mathematical problems as they arise. It is to encourage doing and performing, not studying and pondering what others have done.

I fully expect that, after reading this book, the youngster will find a new enjoyment in mathematics. The adult reader will realize the significance of mathematics in everyday living. All readers should come to appreciate mathematics as more than a topic for esoteric research or a maze of theorems, lemmas, and corollaries. Mathematics is a tool that all of us can use in our daily lives. It can do nothing but help us to become proficient in it.

Chapter 1

Why Machine-Free Math?

At some point, you've probably asked yourself, "Why bother with trying to do math by myself?" You might have reasoned that math is "dirty work" that is somehow below the dignity of your human brain. After all, why should a human brain sweat so hard over something that a machine can do just as well or maybe better? Or you might have been attracted by the nice buttons on a calculator or dazzled by the video screen of a home computer. Perhaps you like these objects and you want to put them to use, so you use them to do your math for you.

Now, I'm not trying to talk you into selling your calculator or your home computer. Machines like these do have their uses. But you may be pleasantly surprised to see how well your mind can actually perform math.

I like machine-free math because it's just plain fun. I prefer to solve a problem without running to some machine for help. To me, working out a math problem with my brain is exhilarating and gives me a feeling of accomplishment. Punching buttons on a calculator is drudgery.

You may object that most math problems you might run across are beyond the ability of your brain to solve. Let me assure you that you are sadly underestimating the power of your brain — even if math is your worst subject. By the time you finish Chapter 3, you will be able to multiply 64 times 46 faster than you could even reach into the drawer to pull out your calculator, let alone punch all those buttons.

But who wants to multiply 64 times 46? Maybe you want to find out how many square feet are in a lot that you want to buy, and the dimensions are 64' × 46'. Or maybe you work in a hotel and you want to make sure that your cash drawer is correct; last night there were 64 rooms occupied at $46 per room.

There are all kinds of people who, for all kinds of reasons, might want to multiply 64 times 46 or something like it. Most of us, when faced with this kind of problem, do one of three things:

1. We decide it really isn't that important, and we really don't care to figure it out anyway;
2. We run for a calculator or even a home computer;
3. (Hurray!) We figure it out ourselves.

The practicality of machine-free math is much greater than most of us realize. For example, machine-free math would allow you to compute your miles-per-gallon quite easily without needing to keep a calculator in your car. Or machine-free math could help you decide which box of corn flakes or what size of pizza is the better buy.

But a small warning is in order here, as long as we're talking about pizza. Remember that a 12″ pizza is really 4 times bigger than a 6″ pizza, since the area of a circle is proportional to the square of its diameter.

Machine-free math can help you out in a lot of places a calculator can't. If the slick and unctuous used car salesman, Rip U. Woff, wants to negotiate loaning you $2,000 and he wants you to pay $160 per month for two years, what kind of interest rate are you getting? Are you going to just sit there and believe that Mr. Woff is giving you a good deal or are you going to check his figures? Unless your calculator can handle logarithms, it won't be able to help you here. But, later in this book, we'll examine the mental math technique that could be used for just this kind of problem.

Suppose you're in an airplane flying from Chicago to San Francisco. The pilot informs you that you are flying over Pinedale, Wyoming at 37,000 feet. It's a nice clear day. If you look out the window on the right side of the plane (binoculars might help), would you be able to see Yellowstone National Park, 75 miles away? Here, a calculator would not help unless it had the ability to use trigonometric functions. But machine-free math could! You could even compute the angle of sighting in time to take a quick look! We'll discuss this type of problem later in the book.

This book consists roughly of two parts. The first several chapters are designed to improve your ability to do purely mental math — that is, math without the need of even paper or pencil. Cultivating this skill will go a long way toward enhancing your enjoyment of machine-free math, since the complexity of problems that you will be able to handle will be dramatically increased.

The second half of the book deals with applications. These are problems that are both practical and fun. For the majority of these problems, you will find paper and pencil a welcome aid.

The possibilities that machine-free math offers are limitless. Machine-free math can be as challenging or as rewarding as you want to make it. No, you won't have to memorize multiplication tables or memorize trigonometric tables. You can do it all with technique and, yes, some practice.

But practice can be fun. When you see an opportunity to solve a problem with mental math, just do it! You're practicing! If you're like me, you'll quickly become amazed at the ability of your own mind to solve math problems.

Now, isn't this more fun than punching buttons? If you agree with me and think it is, then I welcome you to read on. Enjoy the adventure of mental math. Happy figuring!

Chapter 2

You Can Square Anything

You might wonder why I'm starting off with squaring as opposed to something more basic, such as addition or subtraction.

The reason is that everyone knows how to add and subtract. If you want to become better at mental addition or subtraction, just practice on your checkbook for a while.

Squaring, on the other hand, requires technique. There are tricks that can be learned to make squaring any number a relatively simple task. Once you are able to square any number, you can multiply numbers together quite easily. Squaring is a main building block to multiplication, and hence to more complex problems, so far as the scheme of machine-free math goes. So, let's get started.

NUMBERS ENDING IN ZERO

Let's start with numbers ending in 0. They're the easiest. Such numbers can be expressed algebraically as 10t, where t is an integer. From algebra (we'll be using a lot of algebra), $(10t)^2$ expanded gives us $100t^2$. This leads us to the general rule of squaring a number ending in 0.

To square any number ending in 0, first delete the 0, then square the resulting number. Put two zeros on the end of this number for the answer.

Applying this rule to some examples we see that:

$(60)^2 = 3,600$ (Take $6 \times 6 = 36$; add two zeros to get 3,600.)
$(40)^2 = 1,600$, since $4 \times 4 = 16$
$(120)^2 = 14,400$, since $12 \times 12 = 144$
$(200)^2 = 40,000$, since $20 \times 20 = 400$

Get the idea? In the last case, if you didn't know that 20×20 was 400, you could have re-applied the same rule. Thus, since

$2 \times 2 = 4$, $20 \times 20 = 400$, and finally $200 \times 200 = 40{,}000$. This technique is called "nesting" or a "nested sequence," since the same rule may be applied more than once.

But this last point leads us to a more general rule for squaring a number ending in an arbitrary number of zeros.

To square any number ending in an arbitrary number of zeros, first drop the zeros, noting how many were dropped. Then square the remaining number. Put on the end of this number a number of zeros equal to twice the number of zeros that was dropped.

For example:

$(3{,}000)^2 = 9{,}000{,}000$ (Drop three zeros, square 3 to get 9, then add 6 zeros.)

$(90{,}000)^2 = 8{,}100{,}000{,}000$ (Drop four zeros, square 9 to get 81, then add 8 zeros.)

For squaring large numbers (such as in the last example), scientific notation can also be used, if the reader is so inclined. Using this technique:

$(90{,}000)^2 = (9 \times 10^4)^2 = 81 \times 10^8 = 8.1 \times 10^9 = 8{,}100{,}000{,}000$, giving the same result as before with a slightly different method.

So much for numbers ending in 0, at least for the time being. We haven't talked about squaring something like 370 yet, but the method is clear. You would square 37 (to get 1,369, as we will soon see how) and then add two zeros to the end to get 136,900.

NUMBERS ENDING IN FIVE

What about numbers ending in 5? This is the next easiest case. Such numbers can be represented algebraically as $10t + 5$, where t is an integer. Let's apply some rules of algebra and see what happens:

$$(10t + 5)^2 = 100t^2 + 2(10t)(5) + 25$$
$$= 100t^2 + 100t + 25$$
$$= 100(t)(t + 1) + 25$$

You may not realize it right off, but this leads to an extraordinarily simple way of squaring any number that ends in a 5. Before formulating a rule in words, let's apply the above algebraic result to an example. Suppose we want to square 65. In this case, $t = 6$, and $t + 1 = 7$. Applying the formula, we have:

$$(65)^2 = 100(6)(7) + 25$$
$$= 100(42) + 25$$
$$= 4,225$$

Now we are ready to formulate the rule into words.

To square any number ending in 5, first drop the 5, then multiply what is left by itself plus 1. Tack a 25 onto the end.

Let's look at some more examples:

$(15)^2 = 225$ (Drop the 5 to give 1, multiply $1 \times 2 = 2$, add on the 25 to get 225.)

$(45)^2 = 2,025$, since $4 \times 5 = 20$

$(75)^2 = 5,625$, since $7 \times 8 = 56$

$(95)^2 = 9,025$, since $9 \times 10 = 90$

There's no need to limit ourselves to numbers below 100. Try these:

$(135)^2 = 18,225$ $(13 \times 14 = 182)$

$(195)^2 = 38,025$ since $19 \times 20 = 380$

Bigger numbers ending in 5 can also be squared with the same relative ease, but we do not yet have all the necessary tools for doing it. For example, to square 565, you would have to multiply 56×57 to get 3,192 (we'll soon see how this is done), and then tack on the trailing 25 to give 319,225 as the answer.

Knowing how to square numbers that end in 0 or 5 is a big start to knowing how to square anything. This is because any number is very close to a number ending in 0 or 5. As a matter of fact, any number differs from a number ending in 0 or 5 by 2 at the most. This is an important fact in the central idea behind squaring any number at all.

NUMBERS ONE DIFFERENT FROM ZERO OR FIVE

For the next case, let's look at squaring a number that is 1 greater than a number ending in 0 or 5. Examples might be 61 (1 greater than 60), 46 (1 greater than 45), 566, or 2,036. Let's again go back to algebra, and let the letter N stand for a number ending in 0 or 5. We have the following general rule:

$$(N + 1)^2 = N^2 + 2N + 1$$
$$= N^2 + N + (N + 1)$$

The last line is important. Let's look at the example of squaring 61. In this case, let $N = 60$ and apply the formula:

$$(61)^2 = (60)^2 + 60 + 61$$
$$= 3,600 + 121$$
$$= 3,721$$

The rule can now be worded as follows: **The difference between two successive squares is equal to the sum of the two numbers themselves.**

This rule tells us that the difference between $(61)^2$ and $(60)^2$ is $60 + 61$. Similarly, the difference between $(46)^2$ and $(45)^2$ is $45 + 46$, or 91. Thus, $(46)^2$ is just $(45)^2 + 91 = 2025 + 91 = 2116$.

Remember that to apply this rule the numbers must differ by only 1. Here are some other examples:

$$(21)^2 = (20)^2 + (20 + 21) = 400 + 41 = 441$$
$$(81)^2 = (80)^2 + 161 = 6,561$$
$$(96)^2 = (95)^2 + (95 + 96) = 9,025 + 191 = 9,216$$

Notice in these examples that two or more rules may have to be "nested" in order to obtain the final result. Nesting is an intellectually challenging procedure when done mentally because it normally requires some memory. Do some practicing squaring these kinds of numbers. You'll find it a bit difficult at first, but you will soon become quite used to it.

For numbers 1 less than a number ending in 0 or 5, the same principle applies, except this time we need to subtract instead of add. Algebraically:

$$(N - 1)^2 = N^2 - 2N + 1$$
$$= N^2 - N - (N - 1)$$
$$= N^2 - (N + (N - 1))$$

Here are some examples:

$$(59)^2 = (60)^2 - (60 + 59) = 3,600 - 119 = 3,481$$
$$(34)^2 = (35)^2 - (35 + 34) = 1,225 - 69 = 1,156$$
$$(94)^2 = (95)^2 - (95 + 94) = 9,025 - 189 = 8,836$$
$$(199)^2 = (200)^2 - (200 + 199) = 40,000 - 399 = 39,601$$
$$(244)^2 = (245)^2 - (245 + 244) = 60,025 - 489 = 59,536,$$
$$\text{noting that } 24 \times 25 = 600$$

You can see that squaring large numbers is really no different from squaring small numbers, except that some nesting logic must be employed. For example, in the case of squaring 244, the first step was to square 245, a type of subproblem in itself, requiring the multiplication step 24 × 25. Carrying this out to obtain 600, you must then remember why you did it, and thus that 25 must be tacked on to give 60,025. Having completed these steps, you must then remember that it is 244 that you want to square, not 245. So you tuck 60,025 away in memory and work on the next subproblem — that of adding 245 + 244 to get 489. Then you retrieve 60,025 from memory and perform the final subtraction.

The point here is that the method and the principles are basic and hold true, regardless of the size of the number involved. The difficulty in squaring large numbers is only the amount of remembering what must be done while performing the nested operations. Your memory does not have to be vast, but, if necessary, some practice may be in order before you are totally comfortable squaring large numbers.

NUMBERS TWO DIFFERENT FROM ZERO OR FIVE

There remains the class of numbers that differ by 2 from a number ending in 0 or 5, for example 57, 73, 112, 48, etc.

As always, let's revert back to algebra to obtain the necessary result:

$$(N + 2)^2 = N^2 + 4N + 4$$
$$= N^2 + 4(N + 1)$$

Applying this result to squaring 57 (where $N = 55$), we have:

$$(57)^2 = (55)^2 + 4(56)$$
$$= 3,025 + 224$$
$$= 3,249$$

Stating the rule in words, **the difference in the squares of two numbers whose difference is 2 is 4 times the middle number.**

If you are timid about multiplying by 4, perhaps it is easier to do two successive multiplications by 2. Here are some more examples illustrating this principle:

$$(32)^2 = (30)^2 + 4(31) = 900 + 124 = 1,024$$
$$(72)^2 = (70)^2 + 4(71) = 4,900 + 284 = 5,184$$
$$(97)^2 = (95)^2 + 4(96) = 9,025 + 384 = 9,409$$

$(127)^2 = (125)^2 + 4(126) = 15,625 + 504 = 16,129,$
  noting that $12 \times 13 = 156$
$(442)^2 = (440)^2 + 4(441) = 193,600 + 1,764 = 195,364,$
  noting that $(44)^2 = (45)^2 - 89 = 2,025 - 89 = 1,936$

Again, notice the large amount of nesting required to tackle the difficult mental problem of $(442)^2$. Yet it is quite doable! Again, with some practice, even problems of this size will not be hard.

For numbers ending in 3 or 8, the same principles apply as in the above examples, with the difference that we must subtract instead of add. The algebra is as follows:

$(N-2)^2 = N^2 - 4N + 4$
$ = N^2 - 4(N - 1)$

The principle is identical, so we may as well just plunge into some examples:

$(23)^2 = (25)^2 - 4(24) = 625 - 96 = 529$
$(38)^2 = (40)^2 - 4(39) = 1,600 - 156 = 1,444$
$(73)^2 = (75)^2 - 4(74) = 5,625 - 296 = 5,329$
$(148)^2 = (150)^2 - 4(149) = 22,500 - 596 = 21,904$
$(578)^2 = (580)^2 - 4(579) = 336,400 - 2,316 = 334,084,$
  noting that $(58)^2 = (60)^2 - 4(59) = 3,600 - 236 = 3,364$

Squaring 578, as you can see, is a formidable problem to tackle mentally. But, again, it is possible! All it takes is adherence to technique and a little bit of remembering as the nested operations are performed.

There is one more point of methodology that needs to be mentioned with respect to squaring numbers. When squaring a large number that ends in 5, you may find it necessary to multiply a fairly large number by itself plus 1. For example, in squaring 385, you would have to multiply 38 × 39 and then tack 25 onto the end. The multiplication of 38 × 39 is performed by squaring 38 and then adding 38. We can represent this algebraically:
$N(N + 1) = N^2 + N$

In words, **to multiply a number by itself plus 1, square the number and then add the original number.**

Getting back to our problem of squaring 385, our problem becomes one of squaring 38, adding 38, and tacking on a trailing 25. First, to square 38, we notice that it is 2 less than 40. Taking $(40)^2 - 4(39)$ gives us $1,600 - 156$, or $1,444$. Adding 38 gives $1,482$ for 38 × 39. Tacking on the trailing 25 gives $148,225$ for $(385)^2$.

SOME PRACTICE

So that's it — everything you need to know (but were afraid to ask?) about how to square any number at all in your head. We'll conclude this chapter by taking some examples that illustrate all the facets of the methodology, and stepping through the examples exactly as you might in solving the problems mentally.

How about squaring 44? First, we notice that it differs from 45 by 1. The method will be, therefore, to square 45 and then subtract $(45 + 44)$. Squaring 45 gives 2,025. Adding $45 + 44$ is 89. Subtracting $2,025 - 89$ gives 1,936 as the answer.

Let's try squaring 82. We notice that it is 2 more than 80. Hence the method is to square 80 and then add $4(81)$. Squaring 80 gives 6,400; multiplying $4(81)$ gives 324. Adding $6,400 + 324$ gives the answer as 6,724.

For one a little more challenging, let's try squaring 467. We note that this is 2 more than 465. Hence, the method is to square 465 and then add $4(466)$. Both operations are respectable subproblems. Let's start with squaring 465. This requires that we multiply 46×47, and then tack on a trailing 25. Now we must proceed to an even deeper level of nesting, since to multiply 46×47 requires that we square 46 and then add 46. But to square 46, we must square 45 and then add $(45 + 46)$. $(46)^2$ then is $2,025 + 91$, or 2,116. But remember that we really wish to obtain 46×47, so we must add another 46 to 2,116, giving 2,162. Tacking on the trailing 25 gives 216,225, a figure of quite respectable magnitude. But, alas, we are still not done, for we wish to compute $(467)^2$, and must therefore add $4(466)$ to 216,225. If possible, we should tuck 216,225 away in memory, and work on the subproblem 4×466. If we double 466 twice, we obtain 932 and then 1,864. If possible, we would now recall 216,225 from memory to add to 1,864. Assuming you are endowed with a good memory, and are somewhat skilled at mental addition, you will obtain the correct answer of 218,089.

Whew! That one was tough! If you could follow it, you now can square anything.

ADDITION AND SUBTRACTION

I suppose I should say a little about performing the addition 216,225 + 1,864. Mental addition is not easily taught, and perhaps the best way to learn it, as well as subtraction, is to practice balancing your checkbook mentally. But I will suggest a method that I myself use, one that is intuitively simple, but certainly not profound.

What I call the method of decreasing significance works as follows, and it is best illustrated by our example. In adding 216,225 + 1,864, first add 216,225 + 1,000 to obtain the partial sum 217,225. Then add 217,225 + 800 to give 218,025. Then add 60, and finally 4 to obtain 218,085 and finally 218,089. The method gets its name since digits are added one at a time in order of decreasing significance. Partial sums are remembered along the way.

If this method is too slow for you, you can speed the process somewhat by adding the digits two at a time. In our example, you might add 1,800 and then 64, and only require the use of one intermediate partial sum.

The method of decreasing significance can also be used in an analogous manner with problems of subtraction.

So, having said a little about addition, subtraction, and squaring, it's time to call it a chapter. Possibly, you've found that squaring is easier than you thought. If so, then you're well on your way toward becoming a mental math wizard.

Chapter 3

Techniques of Mental Multiplication

If squaring is an exact science with rules and procedures to guide you along your squaring ways, then multiplication is a subtle art. Often, you will find many methods available to solve a given multiplication problem, and you must use some judgment to choose the fastest and/or the easiest.

This book discusses several methods for general multiplication of two numbers. One, the so-called "Old Reliable," is a good general procedure, well suited to mental calculations, and it works quite well. A second method works extremely well for certain classes of problems, and its applicability depends on how well you can square numbers. Several more methods or tricks are also available and will be discussed.

OLD RELIABLE

Let's begin throwing some numbers around by demonstrating how easily you can multiply any number by 10 or less. First, I'm going to assume that you can multiply by 2 quite rapidly. Doubling any number should be easy for you, provided the number isn't so large that you can't remember it all.

How about multiplying a number by 3? All that is involved here is doubling the number and then adding on the original number. But tripling again is easy. We will use doubling and tripling as elementary operations on which more complicated multiplications will ultimately be based.

How about multiplying a number by 4? This operation was used quite a bit when discussing squaring. All that is really involved is two successive doublings. For example, to multiply 346 × 4, double

346 to obtain 692, then double 692 to obtain the answer of 1,384.

Multiplying by 5 is best done by multiplying by 10 and then dividing by 2. An alternate way of looking at the same procedure is to divide by 2 (leaving a decimal .5 if necessary for an odd number) and then multiply by 10. Whichever your preference, you should be able to multiply 69 × 5 to get 345 or 235 × 5 to get 1,175 fairly easily in your head.

Multiplying by 6 gives you a choice. Either you can multiply by 5 and then add the original number, or (easier, I think) you can triple the number and then double the result. Thus, to multiply 78 × 6, you would triple 78 (78 + 78 = 156 and 156 + 78 = 234) to get 234 and then double 234 to get 468. Similarly, to multiply 327 × 6, you would triple 327 to get 981, and then double 981 to get 1,962.

Multiplying by 7 gives another choice. We can either multiply by 5 and then add double the original number, or we can multiply by 6 and then add the original number. I much prefer the second method, which requires remembering just one partial answer along the way. For example, to multiply 87 × 7, you would first triple 87 to obtain 261, then double 261 for 522, and then add the original 87 for 609. On the other hand, the first method requires two separate sub-operations followed by a re-assembly. Eighty-seven would have to be multiplied by 5 to get 435, then again doubled to get 174, and finally the 435 needs to be retrieved from memory to be added to 174 to get the same 609.

Multiplying by 8 simply requires three successive doublings. For example, to multiply 273 × 8, double 273 three successive times to obtain 546, 1,092, and 2,184.

You may guess that the best way to multiply by 9 is through two successive triplings. In fact, it is much easier to multiply by 10 and then subtract the original number. For example, to multiply 66 × 9, multiply it by 10 to get 660, then subtract 66 for the answer of 594.

Theoretically, you could keep going with this general procedure. For example, you could multiply by 11 by multiplying by 10 and then adding the original number; to multiply by 12, you could do successive operations of tripling, doubling, and doubling; and so forth. You could multiply very high with just some elementary operations, like doubling, tripling, and multiplying by 10.

Nice as this might seem in theory, you can see the problem when a larger multiplier is involved. If you needed to multiply by 67, for example, coming up with the correct sequence of multiplying by 10,

2, or 3, and knowing when to add things up becomes the largest part of the problem. Perhaps the easiest way would be to perform six successive doublings (multiplying by 64), and then triple the original number. But designing this algorithm takes more work than executing it.

An easier way would be to notice that, once you can multiply by any number 2 through 9, you can multiply by 20, 30, etc., up to 90. You can also multiply by 200, 300, etc., up to 900.

Now, what if you wanted to multiply by 67? Well, you now know how to multiply by 60, and you know how to multiply by 7, and you know how to add. That's all you need!

Let's try multiplying 24 × 67. First, multiply 24 × 6, which is best accomplished by tripling and then doubling. You would thus obtain 72 and 144. 24 × 60 is then 1,440. To multiply 24 × 7, we don't have to start all over again. We know that 24 × 6 is 144, so 24 × 7 is this plus 24, or 168. The final answer is then 1,440 + 168, which can be gotten through the method of decreasing significance. Proceeding in this way, 1,440 + 100 is 1,540; 1,540 + 60 is 1,600; and finally 1,600 + 8 gives the answer, 1,608.

But there's another way of doing this problem that I think is simpler. Let's multiply 67 × 24 instead of 24 × 67. Now, to multiply 67 × 20 merely involves doubling 67 (134) and adding a 0 to get 1,340. Tuck this away in memory and multiply 67 × 4 by doubling the already computed 67 × 2. Doubling 134 gives 268. Finally, adding 1,340 + 268 gives us the correct answer of 1,608.

You now know "Old Reliable," the first and most basic method used for mental multiplication. Essentially, you multiply by the respective digits of the multiplier and add the results to an "accumulator" of partial sums. The multiplications and additions are performed in an order of decreasing significance.

The biggest question of judgment in this method comes as to the designation of the multiplicand (the number to be multiplied) and the multiplier (the number to multiply by). Generally, the problem will be easier if the multiplier is chosen to be the smaller of the two numbers. This was true in our example, where the better choice for the multiplier was 24 (not 67).

This is not always true, however. Consider 82 × 67. In this instance, 82 is the better choice for the multiplier, since it is easier to multiply by 8 and by 2 than it is by 6 and by 7. This suggests another rule: choose the multiplier as the number with the smaller sum of digits.

Even this rule has numerous exceptions. For example, 132 × 800 is best accomplished with 800 as the multiplier, even though the sum of the digits in 132 is less than in 800.

What it ultimately comes down to is that the choice of multiplicand and multiplier is one of personal judgment. But don't waste inordinate and valuable processing time debating with yourself over which method to use. Even if your choice is wrong, it won't make that much difference.

Some Practice

Let's conclude the discussion of Old Reliable by working out a couple of examples together. For a starter, let's try 43 × 28. If we use 28 (the smaller number) as the multiplier, then the first task is to multiply 43 × 20 to get 860. Store this number in memory. 43 × 8 is best done by three successive doublings to get 86, 172, and 344. Adding 344 to 860 by the method of decreasing significance gives partial sums of 1,160 (860 + 300), 1,200 (1,160 + 40), and 1,204 (1,200 + 4).

Now let's try 88 × 59. Here, we will choose 88 as the multiplier since we can use the result of 59 × 8 for both sub-operations. 59 × 8 can be gotten by three successive doublings, giving 118, 236, and 472. 59 × 80 is then 4,720, and 4,720 + 472 gives the answer of 5,192.

In 94 × 29, let's use 29 as the multiplier. 94 × 20 is easily computed as 1,880. 94 × 9 is best calculated as 940 (94 × 10) minus 94, or 846. Recalling 1,880 from memory and adding it to 846 gives 2,726.

Moving up in the world, let's try 263 × 56. Use 56 as the multiplier, and start by multiplying 263 × 50. Dividing by 2 gives 131.5, multiplying by 10 twice gives 1,315 and 13,150. Store this in memory. To multiply 263 × 6, you can scorn the traditional tripling and then doubling, since we already know 263 × 5 is 1,315. 1,315 + 263 gives 1,578. The answer is then gotten by adding 13,150 + 1,578, best accomplished through decreasing significance. Successive partial sums are 14,150, 14,650, 14,720, and finally 14,728.

As a final illustration of this method, let's look at the problem that became famous in Chapter 1, namely 64 × 46. Let's use 46 as the multiplier. 64 × 40 is best gotten through two doublings of 64 and then tacking on a 0. This gives 2,560. 64 × 6 can be gotten by tripling 64 to give 192, and then doubling 192 to give 384. 2,560 + 384 gives an answer of 2,944. Can you really do this faster than by calculator, as promised? Probably, but if you have any doubts, don't give up. Faster ways of doing this problem are forthcoming.

So with that, let's conclude the discussion of Old Reliable. As the name implies, it's a good solid method that is always doable. Often Old Reliable is the best method, particularly when big numbers (greater than 100) are involved. But there are many instances where trickery can solve a problem much faster than Old Reliable can (although Old Reliable will still do all right).

METHOD OF SQUARES

One class of such trickery has such a widespread applicability that it should really be classed a method by itself. I call this "The Method of Squares." The naming of this method has nothing to do with the personalities of the people who employ it. Rather, it is a slick, streamlined method, extremely useful for a large class of problems. The degree to which this method can be used effectively depends entirely on your ability to square numbers quickly.

Generally, the method of squares works extremely well when multiplying two numbers that are fairly close together and are less than 100. The method is based on the following algebraic relationship:

$$(A + B)(A - B) = A^2 - B^2$$

The crux of the method, then, is to express a multiplication problem as $(A - B)(A + B)$, and then to simply compute $A^2 - B^2$. For some problems, this method is ludicrously simple. For example, 61×59 is quite obviously $(60 + 1)(60 - 1)$. Hence, the desired product is $(60)^2 - (1)^2 = 3,600 - 1 = 3,599$. Likewise, $58 \times 52 = (55 + 3)(55 - 3) = 3,025 - 9$, or $3,016$.

Of course, you won't usually run into problems that are this simple. But if the two numbers are reasonably close together (so that B is readily squared), the method is extremely powerful. Here are some other examples illustrating this method:

$$59 \times 77 = (68)^2 - 9^2 = 4,900 - 4(69) - 81 = 4,900 - 276 - 81$$
$$= 4,900 - 357 = 4,543$$
$$27 \times 83 = (55)^2 - (28)^2 = 3,025 - 784 = 2,241$$
$$141 \times 129 = (135)^2 - 6^2 = 18,225 - 36 = 18,189$$

These examples illustrate the method. In general, the parameter A should be chosen as the midpoint of the two numbers being multiplied; B is then one-half the difference. If B is small, it can be easily squared and subtracted from A^2. Thus, when multiplying two numbers whose difference is small, the problem essentially reduces to one of squaring the midpoint.

To make this method even more useful, if the sum of the units digits of the two numbers is 10, then the midpoint will be a multiple of 5, and hence easily squared. For example, in 78 × 42 (8 + 2 = 10), $(60)^2 - (18)^2$ is the appropriate breakdown, and the answer is easily computed as 3,600 − 324 = 3,276.

What about the famous example of Chapter 1, 64 × 46? We can quickly break this down into $(55)^2 - 9^2 = 3,025 - 81 = 2,944$. I'll bet you can do this faster than you can punch calculator keys!

Avoiding Fractions

All of the examples using this method have so far had one thing in common. All of the multiplications have involved either two even numbers or two odd numbers. This circumstance insures that the two numbers differ by an even number, and that the quantities A and B are integers. A little more thought is required for a problem like 77 × 62. If we break this down into the format of (A + B)(A − B), then we obtain the odious (69½ + 7½)(69½ − 7½), or $(69½)^2 - (7½)^2$. Be careful here! The fractions do not cancel out, leaving you a nice $(69)^2 - 7^2$. If you need to be convinced of this, just expand $(69 + ½)^2$ and $(7 + ½)^2$ algebraically.

We're either stuck with the fractions or we have to look for another approach. Since we all hate fractions, let's look for another approach.

Going back to the original problem, we notice that it is quite close to four other problems that are all in the form we want. If we write 77 as 76 + 1, then (77)(62) becomes (76)(62) + (1)(62). This leads to the problem $(69)^2 - (7)^2 + 62$. Similar problems can be formulated by expressing 77 as 78 − 1, by expressing 62 as 61 + 1, or finally, by expressing 62 as 63 − 1.

Either of these four possibilities will produce a simpler problem than the original, since each creates an even difference between the two numbers that must be multiplied. Which of the four methods of expression should be employed, however, is an interesting question and well-worth looking into.

What we are really trying to do, in terms of making the problem easier, is: One, if possible, pick the numbers in such a way that their midpoint is a multiple of 5, thus making it excessively easy to square. Two, pick the numbers so that their difference is as small as possible so that the second square to be done is as small as possible and easily done; and that the ensuing subtraction involves numbers as small as possible.

With these objectives in mind, let's look at our four possibilities in this manner:

1. Increase the larger number by 1. In our example, this would give us $(78)(62) - 62 = 70^2 - 8^2 - 62 = 4,900 - 64 - 62 = 4,774$.

2. Decrease the larger number by 1. In our example, this would give us $(76)(62) + 62 = 69^2 - 7^2 + 62$ and this is harder than solution one.

3. Increase the smaller number by 1. In our example, this would give us $(77)(63) - 77 = 70^2 - 7^2 - 77 = 4,900 - 49 - 77 = 4,774$.

4. Decrease the smaller number by 1. In our example, this would give us $(77)(61) + 77 = 69^2 - 8^2 + 77$ and this is harder than solutions one (1) or three (3).

Clearly, (1) and (3) are the easiest representations because the squaring is easier. Was this luck that we were able to find such an easy set of numbers to square and subtract? Not really. In the Method of Squares, if the two numbers to be multiplied differ by an odd number, then you have to do some adjusting. You have to employ one of the four methods above, or else abandon the Method of Squares. But the fact that you have four methods available to you is in itself an opportunity to simplify the problem.

I will now show how any multiplication problem involving numbers less than 100 is easy. To see why this is true, let me start by presenting a general algorithm for multiplying any two numbers less than 100. The algorithm is as follows:

If the two numbers differ by an even number, then the Method of Squares can be used with no adjustment necessary. Old Reliable may also be used if the conditions warrant.

If one number is odd and the other even, then:

- If one of the numbers ends in 5 or 0, Old Reliable can be used. Such problems are normally easy by Old Reliable.

- If the units digits of the two numbers add to 9 or 11, then the Method of Squares can be used with an adjustment to make this sum 10. Example: $67 \times 44 = (66)(44) + 44 = 55^2 - 11^2 + 44 = 3,025 - 121 + 44 = 2,948$.

- If the units digits of the two numbers differ by 1, then the Method of Squares can be used with an adjustment to make this difference 0. Example: $78 \times 37 = (77)(37) + 37 = 57^2 - 20^2 + 37 = 3,249 - 400 + 37 = 2,886$.

- If one of the units digits is 1 or 9, and none of the above cases apply, then Old Reliable can be used. Example: $24 \times 39 = (24)(40) - 24 = 960 - 24 = 936$.

This algorithm is complete! There is no multiplication problem that does not fall into one of the above cases. So if you think that the above cases are easy, then multiplication is easy.

Let's try some examples. For 94×63 notice that the units digits differ by 1. Here I would break this up by $(94)(64) - 94 = 79^2 - 15^2 - 94 = 6,241 - 225 - 94 = 5,922$.

For 58×45 I would use Old Reliable. $(58)(40) = 2,320$ and $(58)(5) = 290$, so $(58)(45) = 2,320 + 290 = 2,610$.

For 214×177 notice that the units digits add to 11. So we can use the Method of Squares, expressing the problem as $(213)(177) + 177 = 195^2 - 18^2 + 177 = 38,025 - 324 + 177 = 37,878$.

For 86×32, probably the simplest is Old Reliable. We have $(86)(30) = 1,720 + 860 = 2,580$, and $(86)(2) = 172$. So $(86)(32) = 2,580 + 172 = 2,752$.

For 108×86, the Method of Squares is probably easiest, giving us $(97)^2 - (11)^2 = 9,409 - 121 = 9,288$.

A FEW MULTIPLICATION TRICKS

On to the third method of multiplying two numbers, which can be somewhat loosely termed as "find the trick that works." Here, you look for some inner relationship between the two numbers, or for something unique about one of the numbers. Then you use this information to multiply them together.

One such opportunity for trickery exists when one of the numbers is a multiple, or close to being a multiple, of another number. Algebraically, if the first number is a, and the second number is Na, where N is a constant multiple, the product will be Na^2. Thus, if N is fairly small, and if you're proficient at the squaring operation, this method is easy to employ.

For example, 17 × 34 can be multiplied easily by simply taking $2(17)^2$ or 2(289) = 578. Similarly, 55 × 110 is just $2(55)^2$ = 2(3,025) = 6,050.

Suppose the larger number isn't an exact multiple, but is quite close. The method can still be used. For example, 21 × 86 can be broken down into 21 × 84 + (21 × 2), or further into $4(21)^2$ + 42. Since 21^2 is $(20)^2$ + 20 + 21 = 441, we have 4(441) + 42. 441 is multiplied by 4 by doubling it twice, giving 882 and 1,764. Adding on the 42 gives the answer of 1,806.

As a final example, let's consider 26 × 77. Here, we notice that 26 × 3 = 78, so the problem can be re-expressed as $3(26)^2$ − 26. Squaring 26 gives 676 (625 + 25 + 26); multiplying this by 3 gives 2,028 (add it to itself twice); and finally subtracting 26 gives us the final answer of 2,002.

Another opportunity for trickery exists if one of the numbers is a power of 2, or fairly close to being a power of 2. Since doubling any number is a simple operation, multiplying any number by 4, 8, 16, 32, etc. involves nothing more than successive doublings.

In the problem of Chapter 1, 64 × 46, we notice that 64 is just 2 raised to the sixth power. Hence, six successive doublings of 46 will give us the answer. Proceeding, we obtain 92, 184, 368, 736, 1,472, and finally 2,944. The toughest part of this problem is performing the correct number of doublings.

In 53 × 132, we can break this problem down to (53 × 128) + (53 × 4). To multiply 53 × 128, we need seven successive doublings of 53. These doublings give 106, 212, 424, 848, 1,696, 3,392, and finally 6,784. Adding this to 53 × 4 gives 6,784 + 212, or 6,996 as the final answer.

389 × 16 can be easily performed, similarly, by four successive doublings of 389. Proceeding thus, we obtain 778, 1,556, 3,112, and finally the answer of 6,224.

A third "trick" is called the Upper Roundoff Method. Let's illustrate with the example of multiplying 14 × 98. The easiest way of doing this is to break the problem up into (14 × 100) − (14 × 2). This gives 1,400 − 28 = 1,372 for a quickly obtained answer. Trying to do this problem by Old Reliable, choosing 14 as the multiplier, would not be too bad, but it is more difficult than by this Upper Roundoff Method.

A more interesting use of the Upper Roundoff Method can be seen in the example of 246 × 79. Here, it turns out that the easiest way of doing this problem is to notice that 246 × 80 is not that hard (remember that multiplying by 8 is a quick and easy set of doublings). Thus, we decompose the problem into 246(80) – 246. We multiply 246 × 8 by doubling three successive times to obtain 492, 984, and 1,968. 246 × 80 is then just 19,680. The final problem answer is then 19,680 – 246, or 19,434.

SOME PRACTICE

We will conclude this chapter by taking several general multiplication problems and working them out according to the various methods discussed.

As a starter, let's work out 82 × 67. The numbers are fairly close together, and the units digits add to 9. I would use the Method of Squares, breaking the problem down as 82 × 68 – 82. 82 × 68 is then $(75)^2$ – 49, so we have 5,625 – 49 – 82 for 82 × 67, or 5,625 – 131, or finally 5,494.

Now let's try 94 × 41. Here I'm going to go with Old Reliable, noting that one of the units digits is 1. Choosing 41 as the multiplier, we want to start by multiplying 94 × 40. Doubling 94 twice gives 188 and 376; 94 × 40 is thus 3,760. The answer is obtained by adding 3,760 + 94 to get 3,854.

How about 73 × 149? Here, you might notice that 146 = 2 × 73, and approach the problem from that direction. I would personally prefer the Upper Roundoff Method, treating the problem as 73 × 150 – 73. 73 × 150, a simple problem by Old Reliable, is just 7,300 (73 × 100) + 3,650 (73 × 50), or 10,950. Subtracting 73 gives the answer of 10,877.

In the example 88 × 37, I'm going to use Old Reliable with 88 as the multiplier. 37 × 8 (by three doublings) is 296. 37 × 88 is then 2,960 + 296 = 3,256.

The problem 74 × 23 is again best approached through Old Reliable, with 23 as the multiplier. Performing the multiplication 74 × 20 gives 1,480. Then 74 × 3, by successive additions gives 148 and 222. Adding 1,480 + 222 gives 1,702.

For 95 × 37, I'm going to use the Upper Roundoff Method, decomposing the problem into 37 × 100 – (37 × 5). This gives quite easily 3,700 – 185, or 3,515.

In 122 × 58, let's use Old Reliable with 122 as the multiplier. 58 × 100 gives 5,800 for the first partial sum. 58 × 20 gives 1,160, which we add to 5,800 to obtain 6,960 as the second partial sum. Finally 58 × 2 again equals 116, which we add to 6,960 to obtain 7,076.

How about 44 × 86? Here I would go with the Method of Squares, but the choice is close (Old Reliable with 44 as the multiplier, or 44 × 88 – 44 × 2). The problem thus becomes $(65)^2 - (21)^2$ = 4,225 – 441 = 3,784.

Let's finish up with one hard problem, just so you don't go away too overconfident. We should find sufficient challenge in 263 × 74. This first appears to be approachable only by Old Reliable with 74 as the multiplier. But, I prefer thinking of 263 as 256 + 7, and then recognizing 256 as 2 to the eighth power.

The problem then reduces to eight successive doublings of 74 plus the product 7 × 74. Successive doublings of 74 give 148, 296, 592, 1,184, 2,368, 4,736, 9,472, and finally 18,944. Tuck this away in memory, somehow. To multiply 74 × 7, triple, double, and add. Thus, tripling 74 gives 222; double this for 444; then add 74 for 518. The answer then is 18,944 + 518 or 19,462.

After reading this chapter, you've hopefully realized that multiplication is an art in which choosing the right method for the right problem can make all the difference between fun and confusion.

We haven't talked too much about problems involving numbers greater than 100. In the world of mental arithmetic, these problems come up only seldom, and when they do, you will be prepared for them. If you question your ability to handle these larger problems, don't feel bad. An approximation using corresponding numbers less than 100 is sometimes good enough. For example, 673 × 387 is approximately 67 × 39 × 100.

As a final word, multiplication is an art, and it does take practice. But make your practice fun!

Chapter 4

Division: You Already Know It!

Well, maybe it's not than simple. But, basically, if you know how to multiply, you know how to divide.

A division problem will almost always take you longer than a multiplication problem of comparable difficulty. This is because division uses one algorithm, something like an Old Reliable, and doesn't lend itself well to short-handed trickery and slippery maneuverings. Another aspect that might slow you down is decimal points. A division problem usually demands an answer expressed as a decimal. The answer to the problem 105/10 is better expressed as 10.5 than as 10 with a remainder of 5.

The nice part of division is that conceptually it is easier than multiplication. All you need to do in division is multiply by numbers less than 10 and remember the answer. You don't have to worry about choosing a method, and big numbers aren't nearly so mind-boggling.

GENERAL METHOD

The best way to explain mental division is just to get on with it by doing some examples. Let's start with 52/7, just to illustrate the method. An initial division gives us a quotient of 7 and a remainder of 3. Now, the technique is to add zeros to the remainder, one 0 for each decimal place required in the answer. Let's assume that we wish two decimal places in the answer.

This we can handle in a manner exactly identical to normal long division. First, we divide 30/7 to obtain 4 with a remainder of 2. Finally, we divide 20/7 to get 2 with a remainder of 6. Since the remainder is greater than half of the divisor 7, and since we're computing the last digit of the quotient, we round off the previously computed 2 to a 3. Putting it all together, we have 52/7 = 7.43.

Now that we get the idea, let's try some more challenging problems. 76/13 gives initially a quotient of 5 with a remainder of 11. Dividing 110/13 (appending a 0 to the remainder) gives 8 with a remainder of 6. Finally, 60/13 gives 4, but the remainder of 8 is greater than half of 13, so we'll round up to 5. Now we can put it all together for an answer of 5.85.

As the numbers get larger, the quotients aren't quite so easy to compute. As an example, let's look at 321/47. As a guess at the whole number quotient, let's try 7. Now, to multiply 47 × 7, triple 47 to obtain 141, double this for 282, and add 47 to get 329. We're high by 8. But that's okay. Now we know that the actual quotient is 6 with a remainder of 39 (47 – 8). Now we divide 390/47. Let's estimate the quotient here to be 8. By successive doubling, 47 × 8 is 376. So 8 is the quotient with a remainder of 390 – 376 = 14. For the final division of 140/47, we see that the quotient is very nearly 3. So, putting it all together, we have 6.83.

So far, all of our examples have had quotients less than 10. So let's move up in the world and try a problem slightly more complex. An example might be 3,426/61. First, don't be awestruck by these numbers. Exactly the same principles apply.

Start by looking at 342/61, exactly as you would in long division. You should get a quotient of 5 and a remainder of 37. Now it's too early to start appending zeros, since there's more to the dividend. So the next subproblem is 376/61, proceeding exactly as in long division. This gives 6 with a remainder of 10. Now, appending our first 0, we have 100/61 for a quotient of 1 and a remainder of 39. Finally, 360/61, for our second decimal place, gives 6 with no round-up necessary because the remainder 24 is less than half of 61. Put it all together for an answer of 56.16.

Believe it or not, there really isn't anything more to say about dividing in your head. But it may be worthwhile to discuss here one application of mental division, namely figuring out your gas mileage.

COMPUTING GAS MILEAGE

Gas mileage is an important indicator of engine performance, and it's nice to be able to do this calculation without carrying some machine in your car. Furthermore, you can actually do the calculation in your leisure time while driving or commuting if you keep everything in your mind.

The most common method of computing gas mileage is to do the calculations right at the gas station. According to this method, you simply divide the number of gallons that your car took into the number of miles you traveled since you last got gas.

If you use this method, you may observe erratic and otherwise unexplainable fluctuations in your gas mileage. This is because this method introduces extra variations into the problem.

Due to variations of different gas pumps, human factors, and even physical factors such as temperature and humidity, it is not always possible to "fill it up" consistently. The amount of gas you receive is probably not equal to the amount that your car burned since your last fill-up.

To eliminate this variation, you may rely on your gas gauge, if you believe it is accurate. You can record your mileage, not at the time that you get gas, but at the time your gas gauge reaches a certain level. In my car, my gas gauge consistently indicates a level over "full" when I get gas, so I wait until I drive far enough so that the gauge points exactly to the full indicator. At this point, I compute my miles traveled and my gas mileage. The error coped with in judging the gauge's readings is normally far less than the variations introduced by using the more traditional method.

It may seem silly to go into this discourse, but there is a practical point to be made here. It's pointless to do a division problem to one or two decimal places when the actual result is only likely to be valid to within 20%. So you should try to eliminate all large variations to make the most of your mathematical efforts.

Enough of the theory! Let's start throwing numbers around. Suppose you traveled 313 miles on 14.8 gallons of gas. What's your gas mileage?

What we're looking at is 313/14.8, but decimal points are messy in a divisor. Let's multiply everything by 10 to produce a decimal-point-free problem of 3,130/148. Proceed as in the previous examples, using the same principles.

Our first problem then is 313/148, which gives a quotient of 2 and a remainder of 17. Pulling off the end 0 of the dividend and tacking it onto the remainder of 17 gives us the next subproblem, 170/148. Here we get a quotient of 1 and a remainder of 22. Our next subproblem, 220/148, gives a quotient of 1 and a remainder of 72. Since the remainder of 72 is less than half of 148, no round-up takes place, and your gas mileage is 21.1 miles per gallon.

Well, now you know how to add, subtract, multiply, and divide in your head. You might well ask, "What else is there?" You might well think that there's nothing else to do but practice adding, subtracting, multiplying, and dividing — honing your skills, in other words.

In reality, there's plenty left. As a matter of fact, we've barely scratched the surface of possibilities. So, don't just sit there. Flip the page!

Chapter 5

The Whole New World of Logarithms

To many of us, logarithms are fearful things of higher math. The idea of using logarithms to aid mental calculations would seem unthinkable.

Yet, logarithms really are simple. Many problems involving multiplications and divisions of large numbers are tremendously simplified through the use of logarithms. Logarithms make it possible to undertake certain problems that would otherwise be impossible with or without a machine. Among these are powers and roots, and also the large class of interest rate problems.

Tragically, logarithms have lost some popularity over the past decade as electronic devices have assumed more responsibility for solving problems of mathematics. I was recently shocked to learn that many present-day high school graduates have never heard of logarithms. If you are one of these unfortunates, then do not panic. I will spend a good deal of this chapter explaining the theory and the usefulness of logarithms. Those of you who do know about logarithms may want a review, so there's no need to feel bashful about reading on.

BASIC THEORY

So let's begin by discussing the theory of logarithms. For our purpose, we'll be talking about logarithms to the base 10, since these logarithms are the ones that are useful in machine-free calculations.

Algebraically, we say that a number x is the logarithm to the base 10 of another number y if $10^x = y$. Thus, the logarithm of 10 is 1 ($10^1 = 10$); the logarithm of 100 is 2; the logarithm of 1,000 is

3; and so forth. Similarly, the logarithm of .1 is –1 (since .1 = 10^{-1}); the logarithm of .01 is –2; and so forth. The logarithm of 0 is minus infinity, and logarithms for negative numbers don't exist.

Figure 5-1 is a sketch of the function $\log_{10}(x)$ (hereafter referred to simply as $\log(x)$) versus x.

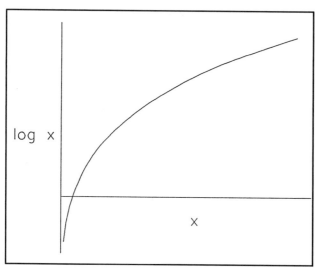

FIGURE 5-1. *Sketch of log x vs. x.*

Right now, you're probably saying, "Yeah, that's fine, but how does all this help me?" The answer to that question is contained in the three laws of logarithms, listed below:

1. When multiplying two numbers together, the logarithm of the product is the sum of the two logarithms of the numbers being multiplied.
2. On dividing, the logarithm of the quotient is equal to the logarithm of the dividend minus the logarithm of the divisor.
3. When raising a number to a power, the logarithm of the result is equal to the logarithm of the original number multiplied by the power to which that number is to be raised.

Rules one and two help simplify multiplication and division of numbers both very large and very small. Rule three makes it possible to solve certain problems with logarithms that would be impossible to solve through means of simple arithmetic.

To understand the theory behind the three laws, all you need to do is go back to the definition of logarithms and recall the rules of algebra relating to manipulations of powers.

It is easy to understand the first law when we recall from algebra that $10^r 10^s = 10^{r+s}$. In this case, we are talking about multiplying two numbers, represented by 10^r and 10^s. The product is 10^{r+s}. Note that the logarithms of the two numbers are r and s, and the logarithm of the product is r + s.

Similarly, the second law can be understood by reverting to the algebra $10^r / 10^s = 10^{r-s}$. Finally, the third law is best represented algebraically by $(10^r)^s = 10^{rs}$.

Notice in the third case that the power s can be any number, and is not limited to being an integer. This fact makes logarithms powerful tools for handling problems involving fractional exponents or roots (as interest rate problems have).

SIMPLE LOGARITHMS

You're probably quite concerned right now, wondering how you're going to compute all these logarithms. Relax! It's easy! To see how, let's start by understanding how to compute the logarithms of all integers less than 10.

Did I say you wouldn't have to do any memorizing? If I did, I was wrong, but not by much. You will have to remember a few logs, from which all others can be deduced. First, you need to remember that log(2) = .301. Next, you'll have to remember that log(3) = .477.

Logarithms of other numbers can then be deduced using the three laws of logarithms.

Since $2^2 = 4$, log(4) = 2log(2) = .602
Since $2 \times 5 = 10$, and log(10) = 1, log(5) = 1 – log(2) = .699
Since $2 \times 3 = 6$, log(6) = log(2) + log(3) = .778
Since $8 = 2^3$, log(8) = 3log(2) = .903
Since $9 = 3^2$, log(9) = 2log(3) = .954

What about log(7)? We can approximate it roughly as being halfway between log(6) and log(8). Going ahead with this approximation, we have (.778 + .903)/2, or .841 as an approximation for log(7). The actual tabled value is .845. You may want to remember the value .845.

Linear Interpolation

This so called "linear interpolation" gets us fairly close, but it is worthwhile to examine the reason for the discrepancy in computing log(7). Recall the shape of the log function from Figure 5-1 and notice that the curve is concave, i.e., it bends downwards. In terms of calculus, the log function has a negative second derivative. What does all this mean? The situation is illustrated in Figure 5-2.

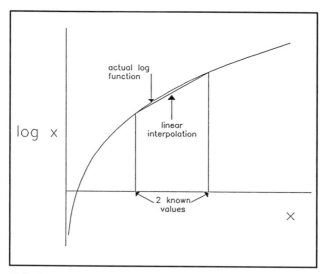

FIGURE 5-2. *Underestimating logarithms by linear interpolation.*

Here you can see that a linear interpolation along the straight line distance between two points will always lie below the real value for a concave function. This is important because linear interpolation will be a key method that we will use for estimating logarithms. So, to be precise, we should "jack-up" by a bit any logarithm estimated by means of linear interpolation. We'll talk more about this later.

CHARACTERISTICS AND MANTISSAS

But alas, it's time to talk about some theory for a bit. You'll need the theory to be able to compute the logarithm of anything.

A logarithm of any number consists of a whole number part, called the characteristic, and a fractional part, called the mantissa. The characteristic is easy to figure out, and can be done by inspection. It is just the whole number portion of the power of 10 that will give the number.

The characteristic of any number between 1 and 10, but not including 10, is 0. Similarly, the characteristic of all two-digit numbers is 1. The characteristic of three-digit numbers is 2, and so forth.

The mantissa, or fractional part, is a little more work, but its estimation is easier if we keep in mind that the mantissa is unchanged if we multiply the original number by 10. Thus, the logarithm of 6 is .778, as computed earlier. Then we have log(60) = 1.778, log(600) = 2.778, and so forth.

A systematic way to compute any logarithm is presented here:

1. Express the number in scientific notation (e.g., $693 = 6.93 \times 10^2$).
2. The power 10 must be raised to is the characteristic.
3. Estimate the mantissa from the portion of the number determined in (1) that lies between 1 and 10. Use linear interpolation.
4. "Jack-up" the logarithm thus determined by a small amount.

Let's illustrate this four-step method with an example. Since we already have a slight start on it, let's compute the log of 693. First, we write this number as 6.93×10^2.

The characteristic is 2, the whole number power to which 10 must be raised. The mantissa is to be estimated from the 6.93 portion of the expression. In fact, the log of 6.93 is, by definition, the mantissa.

We know the log of 6 is .778 and the log of 7 is .845. The log of 6.93 can be estimated then as 93% of the way between .778 and .845, or mathematically as .778 + .93(.845 − .778).

Mentally, we would subtract .845 − .778 to get .067. Now mentally multiply .93 × .067. We can do this by rough guesswork, as about 2/3 of .093 or .062. Then, .778 + .062 is .840, as the approximation for log(6.93).

The jack-up here should be very small, since the linear interpolation error is great only in the middle of an interval (as Figure 5-1 indicates). Here, 6.93 was close to 7, which was one end of our interval. We'll jack it up a bit to .841.

The last step is to add the characteristic and mantissa together to get 2 + .841 = 2.841. The addition of the characteristic and mantissa is an extremely important point. The log of .0693 (6.93 ×

10^{-2}) is not –2.841, as you might be tricked into thinking. Rather, it is $-2 + .841$ or -1.159.

One remaining loose end in all of this is figuring out the amount of "jack-up" in step 4 of the method. Actually, you can probably get by with no jack-up at all most of the time, and just go with the linear interpolation. A bad jack-up can be worse than none at all. But to make you feel a little more comfortable with this nebulous concept, let's try an experiment. We'll compute the logs of all numbers between 10 and 20 using linear interpolation and then compare these calculations to the actual tabled values.

First, we know that the log of 10 is 1.0, and the log of 20 is 1.301 $(\log(10) + \log(2))$. The log of 11 is approximated by $1.0 + .1(1.301 - 1.0)$, or 1.030.

Continuing in this fashion, we obtain the results of Table 5-1.

TABLE 5-1. A comparison of logs approximated through linear interpolation and their actual values.

Number	Log by Approximation	Actual Log
11	1.030	1.041
12	1.060	1.079
13	1.090	1.114
14	1.120	1.146
15	1.151	1.176
16	1.181	1.204
17	1.211	1.230
18	1.241	1.255
19	1.271	1.279

The results of this table are discouraging in terms of the magnitudes of the discrepancies. The largest discrepancy (.026) occurs in estimating log(14). But things are better than they seem.

If we repeat Table 5-1 for numbers from 21 – 29, we obtain far better results. The biggest discrepancy in this range of numbers is a much more tolerable .009. This occurs for 24, where the estimated 1.371 $(1.301 + .4(1.477 - 1.301))$ is not too far from the actual 1.380.

For numbers between 61 and 69, the maximum discrepancy is only .001, and, above the sixties, discrepancies are essentially unnoticeable.

The only problem lies with the numbers 11-19. For this reason, I suggest that you memorize another logarithm, namely $\log(1.5) = .176$. Now we can recompute the logs of 11-19 using a new and more accurate linear interpolation. Now $\log(11)$ would be estimated as $\log(10) + .2[\log(15) - \log(10)]$, and so forth.

When the intermediate $\log(1.5)$ is used, it turns out that the biggest discrepancy in the numbers 11-19 is a mere .009. It's probably worth remembering and using $\log(1.5)$ to achieve the more reliable linear interpolation estimates and to simplify the "jack-up" process.

Jack-Ups

Armed with these results, we can give specific rules for the size of the jack-up. Table 5-2 below gives recommendations for jack-ups to use when the first two digits of the target number are in the range 11-19. Here the reader should interpolate, using $\log(1) = 0$, $\log(1.5) = .176$, and $\log(2) = .301$. Then the jack-up should be applied according to Table 5-2.

TABLE 5-2. Recommended jack-up values to use when computing the logarithm of a target number beginning with the digit 1.

Second digit	Amount of jack-up
1 or 4	.005
2 or 3	.008
6 or 9	.002
7 or 8	.004

Note: A jack-up of zero should be used when the second digit is 0 or 5.

Table 5-3 gives recommended jack-up values for target numbers whose first two digits are in the 20-99 range.

TABLE 5-3. Recommended jack-up values to use when computing the logarithm of a target number with first two digits in the range 20–99.

First digit	Second digit	
	1–3 or 7–9	4–6
2	.006	.008
3	.003	.004
4	.002	.002
5	.001	.002
6	.001	.001
7	0	.001
8	0	.001
9	0	0

Note: A jack-up of zero should be used when the second digit is 0.

Is the jack-up worth it? That's a good question. It depends on how accurate you want to be. If you are satisfied with good approximations, linear interpolation will always work well, will save you a lot of trouble, and will still be good enough to amaze your friends. If you are a true perfectionist, then you need a jack-up.

Throughout the remainder of this book, I will assume you to be a perfectionist, and I will use jack-up values as recommended in Tables 5-2 and 5-3.

SOME PRACTICE

Before continuing, let's calculate some mental logarithms, just to get the hang of it.

Log(35) is estimated as halfway between log(30) and log(40). Log(30) = 1.477 (characteristic is 1 and .477 is log(3)), and log(40) is 1.602 (recalling log(4) = 2log(2) = 2 × .301). The difference 1.602 – 1.477 is .125. Halving this and allowing a jack-up of .004 gives about 1.477 + .067 = 1.544.

Log(138) is estimated as log(100) + (38/50)[log(150) – log(100)], or 2 + .76(2.176 – 2.000) = 2 + .76(.176). We are left with a small multiplication problem. We can guess that .76(.176) is a bit more than ¾ of .176. Since ¾ of .176 is .132, we may estimate our product as about .134. We can then finally estimate log(138) as 2.134, plus a jack-up, or about 2.142.

As a final example, let's look at log(.0056). Here we have a characteristic of –3, which is obvious after rewriting .0056 as 5.6 × 10^{-3}. The mantissa can be estimated by linear interpolation as log(5)

+ .6[log(6) – log(5)] = .699 + .6(.778 – .699) = .699 + .6(.079).

The multiplication of 6 × 79 is accomplished by tripling 79 and then doubling to obtain 237 and then 474. Placing the decimal point gives .047. Adding .699 + .047 gives .746, and adding a slight jack-up gives .748 as the mantissa.

The final answer is the characteristic *plus* the mantissa, or -3 + .746 = – 2.254.

ANTILOGARITHMS

The last problem we shall consider in this chapter is that of taking an antilogarithm. In other words, we want to find the number whose logarithm we are given. Or, going to algebra, if we are given x, we want to determine 10^x.

This problem is important since it is a necessary step in calculations. For example, when multiplying numbers using logarithms, after computing the sum of the logarithms of the two numbers we must find the antilogarithm of that sum to get the final answer.

Taking an antilogarithm is done in exactly the same way as taking a logarithm, except that at the end, we must do a "jack-down" rather than a jack-up. This is because the antilogarithm function, or exponential function, as it is more commonly called, is convex (i.e., curving up or "holding water") instead of concave. Figure 5-3 is a sketch of this function.

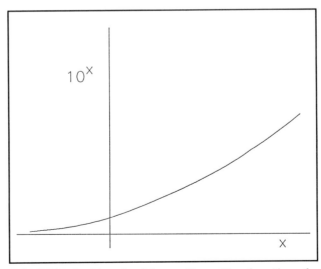

FIGURE 5-3. *Sketch of the antilogarithm function of 10^x vs. x.*

Unfortunately, the antilogarithms that we know are not evenly spaced. We know that the antilogarithm of .301 is 2, that the antilogarithm of .477 is 3, and so forth.

Finding an antilogarithm is best explained through a few examples. As a start, finding the antilogarithm of 3.245 will illustrate the method.

Working with the mantissa, we recall that the antilog of .176 is 1.5, and the antilog of .301 is 2. We need to estimate what fraction of the way between these two lies .245. In other words, we need to compute $(.245 - .176)/(.301 - .176)$, or $.069/.125$.

We can employ our methods of division here by looking at $69/125$. First $690/125$ gives 5 with a remainder of 65. Next, $650/125$ gives 5 with a remainder of 25. Finally, $250/125$ gives 2, and our answer is .552.

We now have $1.5 + (.552)(2.0 - 1.5)$ as our linear interpolation estimation, or $1.5 + .552(.5) = 1.5 + .276 = 1.78$. A slight jack-down gives about 1.76, mindful that we are midway in the region $1.5 - 2.0$.

Finally, seeing that the characteristic is 3 (recall that the original problem was to find the antilog of 3.245), our answer can be expressed as 1.76×10^3 or approximately 1,760.

Now that I've totally confused you, it's time to go back and retrace some of the mysterious steps.

First, notice that we used only three significant digits in the answer (1,760, or 1.76×10^3). This is consistent with our notation throughout the book. It's a misleading display of false accuracy to hold to more than three significant figures when doing linear interpolation.

Jack-Downs

Now, let's talk about the mysterious "jack-down." How did we know to jack-down by .02?

You may think that the amount of jack-down for antilogarithms is related somehow to the amount of jack-up when computing regular logarithms. In fact, the two "jacks" are independent. Table 5-4 gives you a little more of a feel for the amount of jack-down required. It computes the antilogs of .044, .088, and .132 by linear interpolation (antilog of 0 is 1, and antilog of .176 is 1.5) and compares these estimates to the tabled values.

Number	Antilog by Interpolation	Tabled Antilog
TABLE 5-4. Antilogarithms computed by linear interpolation compared to actual values.		
.044	1.125	1.107
.088	1.250	1.227
.132	1.375	1.355

We see that the jack-downs required are on the order of .02. In fact, .02 will in general be the largest jack-down that we will ever need. Again, the jack-downs work on the same principles as the jack-ups do for regular logarithms. The amount of jack-down decreases as the mantissa increases, and is only significant near the middle of an interval.

A simple, approximate rule is to use a "jack-down" of .02 while near the middle of an interval, and 0 otherwise.

One more antilogarithm example is in order, now that we have a little better feel for what is going on.

Let's find the antilogarithm of 4.183. First, we note that the characteristic is 4 and the mantissa is .183. Working with the mantissa, we see that the closest known mantissa values are .176 (the log of 1.5) and .301 (the log of 2). We compute the fraction $(.183 - .176)/(.301 - .176) = .007/.125$. Performing this division mentally (and sparing the details here), we get .056.

Thus our linear interpolation tells us we lie .056 of the way from 1.5 to 2.0, or mathematically $1.5 + .056(2 - 1.5) = 1.5 + .028$, or 1.528. The amount of jack-down will be small, since we are close to the known value of 1.5. Jacking down a small amount and rounding off to three significant figures gives 1.52. Finally, we incorporate the characteristic of 4 to give a final answer of 1.52×10^4, or 15,200.

Again, notice how we carry only three significant digits in the answer. Carrying more would be too presumptuous of us. Where linear interpolations and rough jack-downs are used, we shouldn't pretend too much accuracy.

As a final example, let's compute the antilog of –3.458. As you might have guessed, the trick here is to recognize that the way to break this up is –4 + .542, where –4 is the characteristic and .542 is the mantissa. Remember again that a logarithm is the *sum* of the characteristic and the mantissa, and the mantissa is always positive.

Working with the mantissa of .542, we see that it is bracketed by .477 (log(3)) and .602 (log(4)). We compute the fraction (.542 − .477)/(.602 − .477) = .65/.125 = .520, sparing you the details.

Our estimate is then 3.520 (3 + .520(4 − 3)). Noting it is near the middle of the interval defined by 3 and 4, we select a jack-down of .02, giving us 3.50 when reduced to three significant digits. The characteristic is −4, so our answer is 3.5×10^{-4} = .000350.

LOGS TO OTHER BASES

We'll conclude this chapter with a short discussion of logarithms to different bases. All logarithms of this chapter were to the base 10, quite naturally, since 10 is the logical base for doing arithmetic calculations in our number system.

But you may sometime wish to compute a logarithm to a different base. If so, you will be happy to learn that such logarithms can be computed relatively simply as constant multiples of base 10 logarithms. Looking at the situation algebraically, we can write:

$b^x = y$ where x is $\log_b(y)$.

Now take the log to the base 10 of each side of the equation:

$x\log_{10}(b) = \log_{10}(y)$
or $x = [\log_{10}(y)]/[\log_{10}(b)]$

This formula can be used to compute a logarithm x of any number y to any base b. To do so, compute the logarithm (to base 10) of the number, then divide by the logarithm (to base 10) of the desired base.

You physics and chemistry freaks may occasionally wish to compute a natural logarithm, i.e., to the base e, where e = 2.71828.... To compute a natural log, multiply the base 10 log by 2.303, since $\log_{10}(e)$ = .434 = 1/2.303.

As a last problem, let's solve the equation 23^x = 34,000 for x. In words, we are trying to figure out to what power 23 must be raised to give 34,000. Or, we may express it as finding the log of 34,000 to the base 23.

In any case, by principles just explained, the problem is one of computing the ratio (log(34,000))/log(23).

Let's take log(34,000) first. Expressing it as 3.4×10^4, we see that the characteristic is 4. Since log(3) = .477, and log(4) = .602, the log of 3.4 is approximated by .477 + .4(.602 – .477), or .527. There should be some jack-up since we are in the middle of the approximation interval, so we'll say .531 after jack-up. Combining the characteristic and mantissa gives 4.531 for log(34,000).

Next, we compute log(23). Writing 23 as 2.3×10^1, we see that the characteristic is 1. We recall that log(2) = .301 and log(3) = .477, so the mantissa is approximated by .301 + .3(.477 – .301) or .354. We should jack this up some to about .360. So, we get our approximation for log(23) as 1.360.

The problem then comes down to computing the ratio 4.531/1.360. At this point, we should reduce things down to three significant digits to make the division problem bearable, obtaining 4.53/1.36. Sparing the details, this gives about 3.33 as the final answer.

As you may have noticed, problems involving logarithms can be lengthy. When solving these problems without a machine, it is not a good idea to rush things. Don't look for tricks. Solving the problem, or estimating the solution is important; speed isn't.

As you also may have noticed, the last problem we did could not have been done on many calculators. This is all the more reason to take it slowly and carefully. We're reaching that point where if you make a mistake in your calculations, you may not have a calculator around that'll be able to find your mistake.

Chapter 6

Numbers Both Big and Small

The last chapter dealt with the theoretical aspects of logarithms, what they are and how to compute them, and finally how to take antilogarithms.

PRACTICAL USES OF LOGARITHMS

This chapter will introduce you to the practical uses of logarithms. It turns out that your use of logarithms can place an extremely powerful tool in your mind, so that you will be able to solve many problems which some calculators cannot. For example:

1. Many calculators are not able to operate on numbers greater than 10^8 or less than 10^{-8}. But, through the use of logarithms, you can handle these problems.
2. Most calculators, scientific ones excluded, cannot take powers and roots directly, particularly when fractional exponents are involved. Machine-free math, through the use of logarithms, however, can handle these problems.
3. Only the more sophisticated programmable calculators can handle the vast array of interest rate problems that come up in the life of every individual. Yet again, machine-free math, through the use of logarithms, can handle these problems.

Before we get more specific, it's best to stand aside a bit longer and continue to take in the big picture of logarithms. There are two things that we should always keep in mind when performing calculations involving logarithms.

The first is that logarithms will provide you only with an *approximate* answer. The answer you obtain can be quite accurate but it is never exact. There are several steps in a logarithmic problem that involve slight errors, and the slight errors will tend to increase through the course of the problem. Linear interpolation may not be exact. Performing the jack-up operation is somewhat error-prone. Finally, taking the antilog involves another linear interpolation and a jack-down. That is why, throughout the previous chapter, we have carried around only three significant digits in the answer. Will the answers you obtain by logarithms be accurate to three significant digits? Yes, usually they will be. The techniques taught in the last chapter do lead to accurate approximations if done with care.

The second thing to note here is that logarithmic calculations should always be done with care. Don't rush it. Making a mistake here could throw you off by a factor of 10 or more, and give you an answer that makes no sense. Here, you will have no consolation if you're faster than a calculator. Logarithm calculations are not races. Accuracy is what counts.

MULTIPLYING USING LOGARITHMS

Okay, enough of that stuff. The first problem we'll be talking about will be multiplying two numbers using logarithms. This problem requires the execution of four steps:

1. Find the logarithm of the first number.
2. Find the logarithm of the second number.
3. Add the two logarithms.
4. Take the antilogarithm of the sum.

The answer you will obtain will probably be accurate to three significant figures. Here you might ask if this method of multiplication by logarithms is any better or easier than the conventional methods of Chapter 3.

Let's think about that one. Suppose we have the problem of multiplying $63,487 \times 342$. What if we broke this up into the problem $(6.35 \times 10^4)(3.42 \times 10^2)$, and then used conventional methods? We would have the problem of first multiplying 635×342, then placing the decimal point, and finally reconstructing the exponent of the power of 10.

Personally, I think this problem would be easier if logarithms were used. But perhaps you're still not convinced. Then consider that there are many problems, particularly with scientific applications, that involve successive multiplications and divisions of several large numbers. For example, look at this "monster":

$$(5.72 \times 10^{-7})(2.63 \times 10^{4})(1.96 \times 10^{-2})/(7.67 \times 10^{3})(3.10 \times 10^{-5})$$

Here, logarithms provide the only sensible means of attack. Other than computing five logarithms, the problem would be nothing more than adding and subtracting (and finally computing the antilog).

Performing this problem by conventional multiplications and division would be about where I would draw the line and say that machine-free math really isn't much fun after all. So let's forge ahead and do an example of multiplication through the use of logarithms.

An Example

The first example that we spoke of — 63,487 × 342 — will do fine. We can start by re-expressing this as $(6.35 \times 10^{4})(3.42 \times 10^{2})$, already accepting a small loss of accuracy. Now let's take our time and work this thing out step-by-step and carefully.

Step 1. Find the logarithm of 6.35×10^{4}. The characteristic is 4 and the mantissa is the log of 6.35. To estimate the mantissa, we recall that the log of 6 is .778 and the log of 7 is .845. Linear interpolation gives us .778 + (.35)(.067) as an estimate for log(6.35). The term (.35)(.067) is about $^{2}/_{3}$ of .035, or .023. The log(6.35) is then .778 + .023 = .801 plus a small jack-up to give .802. Log(6.35 × 10^{4}) is then 4.802. Remember that number, or write it down.

Step 2. Find the logarithm of 3.42×10^{2}. The characteristic is 2 and the mantissa is log(3.42). Find the mantissa by recalling that log(3) = .477 and log(4) = .602. Using linear interpolation, we have .477 + .42(.125) as our estimate. To multiply 42 × 125, I would multiply 42 × 1.25 × 100 to obtain 5,250 rather easily. Then we have .477 + .052 or .529 after placing the decimal point and resuming. Adding a moderate jack-up gives us about .533 as the mantissa, and finally 2.533 as our estimate.

Step 3. Add the two logarithms, 4.802 + 2.533. Do this any way you want, but you should end up with 7.335.

Step 4. Find the antilog of 7.335. First, we see that the characteristic is 7. Next, we must find the number whose mantissa is .335. We recall that the log of 2 is .301 and the log of 3 is .477. Our linear interpolation for antilog(.335) is then 2 + (.335 − .301)/(.477 − .301), or 2 + (34/176). Sparing the details, this gives us 2.19. We should allow some jack-down by the methods of the previous chapter, so we'll call it 2.17×10^7 after putting it all together. If you don't like this type of notation, you can write it as 21,700,000.

DIVISION AND POWERS WITH LOGARITHM

Problems of division and of raising numbers to powers follow parallel logic. In dividing, instead of adding the logarithms, we subtract the divisor's logarithm from the dividend's logarithm. In the case of division, however, it is usually easier to perform the operation by the conventional means outlined in Chapter 4. Thus, to divide $(5.86 \times 10^{-5})/(1.48 \times 10^6)$, we might divide $5.86/1.48$ conventionally to obtain 3.96. The appropriate power of 10 is gotten by subtracting $(-5 - 6)$. Thus, the solution is 3.96×10^{-11}.

Problems of raising numbers to powers can be treated in a way parallel to multiplication using logarithms. Here, the log of the original number is multiplied by the power to obtain the logarithm of the answer. This method will be illustrated in depth when we consider interest rate problems.

You're probably wondering how we did when we multiplied $63,487 \times 342$. How close were we to the right answer?

Well, I suppose I could check it. Surprising as it may seem, I actually do have a calculator. But it's lying someplace on the other side of the room in the bottom of a dusty drawer. I'm not exactly sure where it is, to tell you the truth, and the batteries may need recharging.

Still, I guess if I really wanted to, I could walk over there and get it. But I really don't want to bother. I would much rather continue writing this book.

Chapter 7

When Accuracy Really Counts

The title of this chapter may surprise you if you are content with the three-figure accuracy obtained in logarithm calculations so far.

Actually, three-digit accuracy is pretty good. But there are other kinds of logarithm problems where we probably won't get anything close to three-digit accuracy unless we change our method somewhat.

ERRORS IN USING LOGARITHMS

Let's take a moment to analyze the sources of errors that come about in problems such as those of Chapter 6. There will always be some small error in estimating logarithms by linear interpolation, mostly due to the guessy jack-up procedure. When we estimate two logarithms in this way and then combine them by either addition or subtraction, one of two possibilities can happen.

First, the errors in the two logarithms can be such that they cancel each other out in addition or subtraction. In this case, the total error will be very small. The second possibility is that the errors will add. Then the total error becomes noticeable, but usually is still tolerable.

Now, imagine raising a number to a power using logarithms. This would require estimating the logarithm, then multiplying this logarithm by the power, and finally finding the antilogarithm.

The power involved may be large, as is typical in many problems, particularly interest rate problems. Here, the error in estimating the logarithm will multiply itself several times and produce an unacceptably inaccurate final answer.

So to continue to use logarithms effectively in more advanced problems, we need an alternative estimation scheme, one that will perform better than linear interpolation and jack-up.

The answer will come to us from calculus, and it will involve an application of Taylor Series. But before we go plunging into this new concept, it will do us good to discuss some basic ideas of calculus, which lead to the development of the Taylor Series.

A LITTLE CALCULUS

We want to talk about a branch of calculus called "differential calculus." Differential calculus is concerned with determining rates of change. Given a function, say a graph of y vs. x, differential calculus tries to figure out the rate of change of y with respect to x. Let's look at an example.

Figure 7-1 is a sketch of the curve $y = x^2$. Notice how the curve initially decreases, then levels off, and is actually flat when $x = 0$. Then it begins to slope up at an increasing rate.

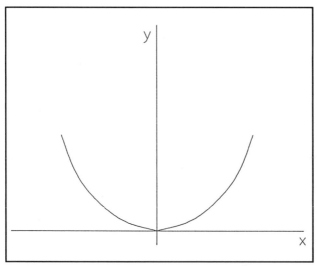

FIGURE 7-1. *Sketch of the function $y = x^2$.*

If we would like to rigorously measure the rate of change of y with respect to x along each point of the curve $y = x^2$, we would approach this problem something like this: For a large number of points along the curve, geometrically construct the straight line that is tangent to the curve at each selected point. Measure the slopes of each of these lines, which give the rates of change of y with respect to x at each selected point.

If we were to compute a large number of these rates of change, and then graph them, we would obtain a straight line as in Figure 7-2.

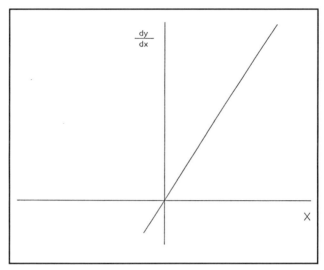

FIGURE 7-2. *Sketch of the first derivative of the function y = x².*

Notationally, we refer to the rate of change of y with respect to x as dy/dx. We also refer to this function as the first derivative.

The line in Figure 7-2 has an intercept of 0, since the rate of change of y with respect to x in the $y = x^2$ curve is 0 when x = 0. We can measure the slope of the line of Figure 7-2. We would find it equal to 2. Hence, the line of Figure 7-2 has the equation y = 2x.

We could now continue and ask, "What is the rate of change of the rate of change?" We can answer this question at once by referring to the line of Figure 7-2, and noting that this line has a constant slope of 2. Then, the second derivative (i.e., the rate of change of the rate of change) is equal to a constant of 2.

Similarly, the third derivative, equal to the rate of change of the second derivative, is 0, since the second derivative is unchanging. Likewise, the fourth and higher derivatives are also all 0.

In the world of calculus buzzwords, we say that the first derivative of x^2 is 2x, the second derivative of x^2 is 2, and the third and higher derivatives are 0. (For a discussion of the theory of derivatives and how to find them, see Appendix A.)

THE TAYLOR SERIES

With that background, we're now ready to discuss some specifics of the Taylor Series. The motivation behind the Taylor Series is that we wish to compute a functional value that is close to one we already know. For example, knowing $(60)^2$, we could compute $(61)^2$ by means of the Taylor Series, or knowing log(2), we could compute log(2.1).

The Taylor Series theory is based on looking at rates of change. It is actually an infinite series, containing one term for each derivative. The terms of the infinite series grow rapidly smaller, however. In practical calculations, it is unlikely to use more than three terms, and almost never more than four.

The form of the Taylor Series is as follows:

$$f(x + y) = f(x) + f'(x)y + f''(x)y^2/2! + f^3(x)y^3/3! + f^4(x)y^4/4! + \ldots$$

(Equation 7-1)

What is going on here? Let's take some time out to explain these mysterious symbols.

First, x and y are variables, with the spirit that y is much smaller than x. The symbol f refers to the functional value. When we are referring to the function x^2, for example, x may be 60 and y may be 1; then $f(x) = 60^2$ and $f(x + y) = (60 + 1)^2$.

The symbol $f'(x)$ refers to the first derivative of the function evaluated at x. Again, for the function x^2, $f' = 2x$ as discussed earlier. If x = 60, then $f'(x) = 2(60) = 120$. Similarly, the symbols $f''(x)$, $f^3(x)$, and $f^4(x)$ refer to the second, third, and fourth derivatives of the function evaluated at x.

Finally, the exclamation point refers to the factorial operation. Thus, $2! = 2 \times 1 = 2$, $3! = 3 \times 2 \times 1 = 6$, $4! = 4 \times 3 \times 2 \times 1 = 24$, and so forth.

So, let's try it out. Let's compute $(61)^2$ using a Taylor Series, just so you see how the method works. For this problem, we will use x = 60, y = 1, and we also have $f = x^2$, $f' = 2x$, $f^2 = 2$, and $f^3 = 0$. Evaluating for x = 60, we have $f(x) = 3,600$, $f'(x) = 120$, $f^3(x) = 2$, and $f^4(x) = 0$. Now plug everything in, and see what we get:

$$(61)^2 = 3,600 + (120)(1) + (2)(1)^2/2 + (0)(1)^3/6 + 0$$
$$(61)^2 = 3,600 + 120 + 1 = 3,721$$

And there you have it! We have the right answer, as I'm sure you can quickly check by $(60)^2 + 60 + 61$ from the methods of Chapter 2.

Notice two things:

1. The terms of the third and higher derivatives were all 0, since those corresponding derivatives were all 0;
2. The terms rapidly get smaller. In fact, we could have had an excellent estimate of 3,720 by just looking at the first two terms, which are extremely easy to compute.

Now we're ready to move on to bigger and better things. Let's look at the Taylor Series applied to estimating logarithms. First, you need to know the derivatives of the logarithm function. The first few are as follows:

$f(x) = \log_{10}(x)$
$f'(x) = .434(1/x)$
$f''(x) = .434(-1/x^2)$
$f^3(x) = .434(2/x^3)$
$f^4(x) = .434(-6/x^4)$

Can you see the pattern? In general, the sign of the n-th derivative will be positive for odd derivatives and negative for even ones. The magnitude (i.e., ignoring the sign) of $f^n(x)$ is $.434((n-1)!/x^n)$.

You may wonder what the mysterious .434 factor is doing there. It turns out that .434 is the logarithm to the base 10 of e (where e = 2.71828 . . . and is the base of natural logarithms). We would not need this extra factor if we were dealing in natural logarithms.

Now let's try an example. We'll compute log(2.1), using log(2) = .301 as a starting point. Using x as 2 and y as .1, the derivatives are as follows:

$f(x) = \log(2) = .301$
$f'(x) = .434(1/2) = .217$
$f''(x) = .434(-1/4) = -.109$
$f^3(x) = .434(2/8) = .109$
$f^4(x) = .434(-6/16) = -.174$

Now, plug everything into the Taylor Series formula:

$\log(2.1) = .301 + (.217)(.1) - .109(.01)/2 + .109(.001)/6 - .174(.0001)/24$
$\log(2.1) = .301 + .022 - .001 = .322$

Since we are computing to three significant figures, the third and fourth derivative terms may be considered so small that we won't consider them. Notice again that a very good estimate is obtained with only the first two terms of the Taylor Series (the $f(x)$ and $f'(x)$ terms).

What about using the Taylor Series method for machine-free calculations? First, let's keep in mind that we only need three significant digits in our answer. In that case, we will never need to compute any more than the first three terms of the series. The largest that the fourth term (the third derivative term) can ever be in our log calculations is considerably less than .0005.

So for our purposes in computing logarithms, we can greatly simplify the Taylor Series formula to include only the first three terms. Thus, we obtain the Taylor Series specially suited for computing logarithms:

$$\log(x + y) = \log(x) + .434(y/x) - .217(y/x)^2$$

It is possible to combine the second and third terms of this formula:

$$\log(x + y) = \log(x) + .217(2(y/x) - (y/x)^2) \qquad \text{(Equation 7-2)}$$

This form is highly recommended for machine-free calculations since it minimizes the number of multiplications required. Let's try it out on some examples.

Some Practice

To compute $\log(356)$, we see that the characteristic is 2, and the mantissa is the log of 3.56. We will use the Taylor Series to compute the mantissa. Here, $x = 4$ and $y = -.44$.

Continuing, we have $y/x = -.44/4 = -.11$; and $(y/x)^2 = (-.11)^2$, or .012 (keeping three significant figures). Then, $2(y/x) - (y/x)^2$ is $2(-.11) - .012 = -.232$.

Next, we are left with $-.217(.232)$. Here, I would suggest multiplying 217×232 using the Method of Squares to give the problem $(225)^2 - 7^2 - 232 = 50,625 - 281 = 50,344$. Then, placing the decimal point, we have .050, rounding to three significant digits.

We're left with $\log(4) - .050$, remembering that the sign of $(.217)(.232)$ was negative. This gives $.602 - .050 = .552$ as the mantissa. The final estimate for $\log(356)$ is 2.552.

The actual tabled value for log(356) = 2.551450. The sources of our small error were two: first, our product of .217 × .232 = .050344 was rounded to .050, producing an error of .000344. Second, the number 3.56 was almost midway between 3 and 4, where the third derivative term would have the largest effect, if it were included.

As a second example, we can try log(6,187). Here we see that the characteristic is 3 and the mantissa is log(6.187). To compute the mantissa, we will employ the Taylor Series with x = 6 and y = .187. Plugging everything into the formula, we have:

$$\log(6.187) = .778 + .217(2(.187/6) - (.187/6)^2)$$

Start by dividing .187/6 to obtain .031. Then .031 squared is .001, when rounded to three significant figures. Computing the parenthetical expression gives 2(.031) - .001 = .061.

Now to multiply .217(.061). This is best done by Old Reliable to obtain .013. Add this to .778 and then add the characteristic to get the final answer of 3.791. The tabled value is 3.79148.

Taylor Series usage has the advantage of being very accurate and reliable, and consistently so. It may be slightly more difficult than linear interpolation, but you avoid the amorphous guesswork associated with "jack-up" factors. I would always recommend that you use this method when accuracy is important, particularly when you are raising numbers to powers.

TAYLOR SERIES AND ANTILOGARITHMS

You may have thought up a good question right about now. What about using Taylor Series theory to estimate antilogarithms? This is a good question.

You can use Taylor Series in this instance, as we will study in the next few pages. But its use in computing antilogarithms is not crucial. If you are computing a logarithm and then multiplying the logarithm by a high power, it is important to minimize the error in the original logarithm estimate. Computing an antilogarithm, conversely, is the final operation of a problem, and errors in estimating antilogarithms do not multiply or propagate.

Nonetheless, when striving for accuracy and not worried about a little extra effort, then the Taylor Series is an excellent method for computing antilogarithms.

Let's look at how this method would work. First, note that the antilogarithm of a number x is really 10 raised to the power x. The derivatives of this function are as follows:

$f(x) = 10^x$

$f'(x) = 2.30(10^x)$

$f''(x) = (2.30)^2(10^x)$

We will ignore third and higher derivatives, since, for our purposes, the corresponding terms of the Taylor Series will be negligibly small. The "mystery" factor 2.30 is actually the natural log of 10. If we were dealing with the function e^x, instead of 10^x, this extra factor would not be present.

Now let's go back to the form of the Taylor Series and write a form to apply to the antilogarithm function. We have:

$$10^{x+y} = 10^x + 2.3(10^x)y + 2.65(10^x)y^2 \qquad \text{(Equation 7-3)}$$

where 2.65 was obtained by combining $(2.30)^2/2!$.

As an example, let's find the antilog of 1.643. We recognize the characteristic as 1 and the mantissa as .643. Focusing on the mantissa, we recall that log(4) = .602 and log(5) = .699. So, we'll choose x = .602 and y = .041 to plug into the Taylor Series.

We have $10^x = 4$, and $y^2 = .001641 = .002$, maintaining three significant figures.

Now we can stick all the numbers into the equation to get:

$$10^{.642} = 4 + 2.3(4)(.041) + 2.65(4)(.002)$$

Sparing you the details, when the dust clears we finally wind up with $10^{.643} = 4.398$, and our final answer for the antilog of 1.643 is 43.98. This agrees exactly with the tabled value.

The Taylor Series methods are decidedly more arduous than simple linear interpolations. You may only want to use Taylor Series approaches when you have paper and pencil handy.

Chapter 8

Powers and Roots

The first time that I was ever called a math wizard was when I was estimating the square root of a large number without paper or a calculator. Of course, you really don't need to be a wizard to do all this. Once you have a familiarity with logarithms, the problem becomes much simpler than the ordinary person could ever guess.

And yet there is something awe-inspiring about performing a feat in your head that most people could not do with paper. If you are into being a show-off, then this chapter is dedicated to you. Nothing will increase your reputation as a math wizard more than doing a few powers and roots in your head. Of course, you don't want to get too carried away with things. If you start computing aloud the cube root of 85,000 in the middle of a crowded restaurant, it's true that you will appear intelligent. But you'll also get a lot of strange looks.

If you're not into showing off, then I'm with you. The real reasons for mental math is fun, enjoyment, a sense of personal achievement, and just a dash of practicality. Computing powers and roots mentally offers all these things.

A LITTLE ALGEBRA

We'll get started into this interesting subject by first reviewing the relevant rules of algebra. When raising a number to a power, the power is referred to as the exponent. An exponent can be either positive, negative, or 0; it can also be either rational or irrational (or non-real, as some readers may correctly point out, but this last case is beyond the scope of this book). Explanations of the significance of these categories are as follows:

1. A number being raised to a positive integer exponent is multiplied by itself a number of times equal to the value of the exponent.

2. A number being raised to a negative exponent is the reciprocal of the same number raised to the corresponding positive exponent, e.g., $x^{-4} = 1/x^4$.

3. Any number being raised to an exponent of 0 is equal to 1.

4. Any number being raised to a fractional exponent is first raised to the power indicated by the numerator, and then the root indicated by the denominator is taken. For example, 4 raised to the power 3/2 is equal to the square root of 4^3, or 8. The root can be taken first if desired, so the same problem can also be computed as two cubed (since 2 is the square root of 4).

5. We can also raise a number to an exponent that cannot be expressed as a fraction. Such exponents are the transcendental functions and other quantities such as sin ($56°$), π (= 3.1415926...), e (= 2.17828...), etc. These are legitimate quantities that cannot be expressed as a finite decimal or repeating decimal, and therefore cannot be expressed as the ratio of two integers. How then to handle these problems? The only thing we have to fall back on is logarithms. We would multiply the logarithm of the base by the exponent to obtain the logarithm of the result.

In machine-free calculations, regardless of the kind of exponent we are dealing with, we always use one method: multiply the logarithm of the base by the exponent to obtain the logarithm of the answer.

SOME PRACTICE

That's all there is to it. That's all there is to talking, that is. Now it's time to start flinging numbers around. The examples that we'll do in this chapter will all utilize the Taylor Series approximations, not because that method is always the most practical, but because with practice this method can become more accurate than other methods.

The Taylor Series equations 7-2 and 7-3 from Chapter 7 are copied here for easy reference:

$\log(x + y) = \log(x) + .217(2(y/x) - (y/x)^2)$ (Equation 7-2)

$10^{x+y} = 10^x + 2.3(10^x)y + 2.65(10^x)y^2$ (Equation 7-3)

Let's begin by computing the cube root of 186,700. First, we express this problem mathematically as $(1.867 \times 10^5)^{1/3}$.

As step 1, we compute the logarithm of 1.867×10^5. We note that the characteristic is 5 and the mantissa is $\log(1.867)$. Now we'll work on the mantissa. We'll use Taylor Series with $x = 2$ and $y = -.133$. We plug these numbers into equation 7-2 above and see that we should start by computing y/x, or $-.133/2 = -.067$. Then $(y/x)^2 = .004$, which we shall round off to 0.

This leaves us with the computation $\log(1.867) = .301 - .434(.067)$.

The multiplication of $.434 \times .067$ gives $.029$, sparing you the details. So, we have for $\log(1.867)$ an estimate of $.301 - .029 = .272$. Now, the log of 186,700 is just 5.272, after adding in the characteristic.

Now for step 2. Multiply the logarithm of the base (5.272) by the exponent (1/3). This operation gives a value of 1.757 as the logarithm of the answer.

The final step is to take the antilogarithm of 1.757. We separate out the characteristic (1), and take the antilog of the mantissa (.757). To do this, we'll use Equation 7-3 with $x = .778$ (whose antilog is 6) and $y = -.021$. We plug these values into the Equation 7-3:

$$10^{.757} = 6 + 2.3(6)(-.021) \text{ since } y^2 \text{ term rounds to } 0.$$

Sparing you the details, we obtain 5.71 as our antilog. Finally, recalling that the characteristic was 1, we obtain as the solution 5.71 $\times 10^1$, or 57.1. It was a lot of work, but the answer is precise.

As a second (and final) example, we'll compute the value of 73 raised to the power of 3.4.

First, we express this mathematically as $(7.3 \times 10^1)^{3.4}$ and then proceed along exactly the same lines as in the previous example.

So, as our first step, we need to compute the log of 7.3×10^1. The characteristic is 1 and the mantissa is $\log(7.3)$. We estimate this mantissa by the Taylor Series Equation 7-2 with $x = 7$ and $y = .3$. We then have $y/x = .3/7 = .043$, and $(y/x)^2 = .002$.

Continuing, we have $\log(7.3) = .845 + (.217)(.086)$, where $\log(7) = .845$. We can multiply $.217 \times .086$ by Old Reliable. This multiplication gives $.019$, and $.845 + .019 = .864$ as our estimate for $\log(7.3)$. Then we have 1.864 for $\log(73)$.

For step 2, we multiply this logarithm by the exponent, giving us the problem 1.864×3.4. Here, I would round 1.864 to 1.86 and multiply 186×34 by Old Reliable to obtain 6,354; place the decimal point for 6.354. What about our round-off, dropping 1.864 to 1.86? We can check by multiplying .002 (the amount of the roundoff) by 3.4, and see if it's worth worrying about. It gives .0068, which is significant. We'll add it to 6.354 to obtain 6.361.

Now for step 3. Take the antilog of 6.361. The characteristic is 6 and the mantissa is .361. To compute the antilog of .361, use the Taylor Series Equation 7-3 with x = .301 and y = .060. Plug it all in like this:

$$10^{.361} = 2 + 2.3(2)(.060) + 2.65(2)(.0036)$$
$$= 2 + .276 + .019$$
$$= 2.295.$$

Recalling that the actual logarithm was 6.361, our final answer is then 2.295×10^6 or, if you prefer, 2,295,000.

TAYLOR SERIES IS NOT SIMPLE

Whew! Taylor Series calculations are not easy. You're probably wondering if Taylor Series is worth so much work.

Well, I'm not going to try to force it down your throat. I'm not going to defend it like a champion either. In the examples of this chapter, I'll admit that linear interpolation would have been a lot easier. And, unless we really need to be super accurate in computing $(73)^{3.4}$, linear interpolation would have done just fine.

In the next chapter, we'll be talking about interest rate problems. This class of problems provides an excellent forum for Taylor Series. These problems require the accuracy that only the Taylor Series method can provide, and the good news is that they make calculations by Taylor Series easy because of the nature of the numbers involved.

So, don't despair with the Taylor Series methods. They are extremely powerful tools. And if they are too much to handle mentally, don't be afraid to use some paper.

Interest Rate Problems

All problems that involve a sizeable investment or expenditure of money and require borrowing money have to do with interest rates. Dealing with interest rate problems is a necessary course in every person's life. Sooner or later, you will need to buy a new car or a house, or perhaps you will just want to pursue some new investment avenue.

IMPORTANCE OF INTEREST RATES IN DAILY LIFE

Your decisions in these matters should be based to a large extent on interest rate analysis, since significant purchases involve large amounts of borrowed money. If you are considering spending $80,000 or more on a new house, for example, this investment will have a considerable influence on your life. Therefore, would you not agree that it is worth taking some time at the outset to analyze the decision?

I am always amazed by those who will spend extra hours out of their weekends hunting for bargains at supermarkets, trying to save a few dollars a month. But these same people, when faced with a truly big money decision, such as buying a house, will not take the time to make an intelligent decision but will act on the basis of impulse and emotion.

Interest rate problems form the basis for the most important decisions in our lives, yet very few of us understand the basic mathematics behind them. Can you do interest rate problems? Can you write a program to do them on your personal computer, or can you program your calculator to do them? Can you do them with paper and pencil? Lamentably, most of us have to answer no to all of these questions.

Interest rate calculations are based on the manipulations of logarithms. They normally require raising numbers to powers, sometimes large powers. Hence, Taylor Series estimating procedures are highly recommended here. Sometimes roots must be extracted.

In this chapter, we will concentrate on five problems, each of which has a definite practical application. These five problems are:

1. Compound interest. If you deposit a certain amount of money in a savings account with compound interest, how much will it become worth in time?
2. The IRA problem. If you deposit $2,000 per year in an IRA until retirement, how much money will you eventually have? How much will you be able to withdraw per month at retirement in order for your funds to last fifteen years? And how much will you save by not having to pay taxes on the interest income during the accumulation period?
3. The used car salesman of Chapter 1. If you are offered a loan for so much money, with constant monthly payments for a certain number of years, what is your actual rate of interest?
4. The house payment problem. If you want to buy a house for so much money at a given interest rate over a certain number of years, what will your payments be?
5. The problem of alternative investments. Given two investments of differing cash flows, which one would be preferred to the other?

As you can see, these sample problems form a broad base for all interest rate problems. Following and understanding the solutions and methods used in these examples will give you an understanding of the theory of these problems, as well as show you how to compute them.

Let's start off with the easiest one of the five.

COMPOUND INTEREST

Suppose you deposit $10,000 in a long-term, time-deposit savings plan. Suppose the plan guarantees 12% annual interest compounded quarterly. How much will you have after five years — the length of the plan?

The formula to use for this calculation is:

$$M = (1 + i)^n \qquad \text{(Equation 9-1)}$$

where M = the multiplier, i.e., by what factor your money will multiply.

i = the interest rate per period (in this case .03, which is 12% spread out over four quarters).

n = the number of periods (in this case twenty, since there are four compounding periods per year and five years in all).

Notice that the parameters i and n have values based on the *compounding* period, in this case once every three months.

So, we now have:

$$M = (1 + .03)^{20} = (1.03)^{20}$$

We know how to compute this. We find the log of 1.03 by Taylor Series, then multiply it by 20, and finally find the antilog.

We find the log of 1.03 by using x = 1.0 and y = .03 in our Taylor Series formulation. This formula (Equation 7-2) is repeated here for convenient reference:

$$\log(x + y) = \log(x) + .217(2(y/x) - (y/x)^2)$$

Here $y/x = .03$ and $(y/x)^2 = .0009$. Then the parenthesized quantity $2(.03) - .0009 = .06 - .0009 = .059$ when three significant figures are used.

Since x = 1 and log(x) = 0, we have:

$$\log(1.03) = .217(.059)$$

One way to compute this is by the method of Upper Roundoff, as 217 × 60 – 217, or 13,020 – 217 = 12,803. Place the decimal point and round to three significant figures to obtain log(1.03) = .0128.

Now we multiply (.0128)20 to obtain .256 as the log of the multiplier M.

The next step is to find the antilog of .256 by Taylor Series. The formula (Equation 7-3) is repeated here for easy reference:

$$10^{x+y} = 10^x + 2.3(10^x)y + 2.65(10^x)y^2$$

In the case of .256, we choose x = .301 and y = −.045. Plugging the numbers gives us:

$$10^{.256} = 2 + 2.3(2)(- .045) + 2.65(2)(.002025)$$
$$= 2 - .207 + .011$$
$$= 1.804$$

This is our value for the multiplier M. In other words, your money will multiply by a factor of 1.804. Recalling that your original deposit was $10,000, this means that you will have approximately $18,040 after the five years.

Taxes and Inflation

Do you sense a bit of academic unreality in this problem? Have we maybe, just possibly, left out something or forgotten about someone? Hint: his initials are U.S. and the "U" stands for "Uncle." Right! What about taxes?

First, you need to know your marginal tax rate. This is the rate at which your extra income will be taxed. Let's assume that this rate will stay constant during the five-year period, since to assume otherwise would be too presumptuous.

Let's assume that your marginal tax rate is 40%. Then the after-tax interest rate that you see is not 12%, as in our original problem, but only 60% of 12%, or 7.2%. The other 4.8% is paid to the government and cannot be accumulated or compounded. Now, how much money will we have after the five years?

The problem is the same, except that we have a new value for i in the equation for M. We have:

$$M = (1.018)^{20}, \text{ where } .018 = .072/4$$

The problem is solved in exactly the same manner. We find the log of 1.018 as .0078. We multiply by 20 to get .156 as the log of M. We can take the antilog, using log(1.5) = .176 to give us an x = .176 and y = −.020 for the Taylor Series equation.

The final answer is $14,330. In other words, the taxes amounted to $3,710 in all, considerably more than a simple 40% of the would-be profit of $8,040.

Have we still forgotten something? What about inflation? At the current stage of writing this book, inflation is at 6%.

Your entire 12% gets taxed down to 7.2% actual after-tax profit. We are actually beating inflation then by 1.2% per year, since 7.2% − 6% = 1.2%.

Recomputing the problem on this basis gives:

$$M = (1.003)^{20} \text{ where } .003 = .012/4.$$

Sparing you the details, the result is $10,616, for an after-tax, after-inflation profit of $616 for investing $10,000 over five years.

Some readers may have heard of the so-called "rule of 72" for estimating compound interest over a number of years. Simply stated, this rule says that your rate of interest, expressed as a percent, divided into 72, will give you the number of years for your money to double. For example, a constant annual rate of return of 8% would let you double your money in about nine years.

This rule is simple and surprisingly accurate. Why does it work?

It is just a special case of Equation 9-1, setting M = 2. This gives us:

$$2 = (1 + i)^n$$
$$\log(2) = n \log(1 + i) \qquad \text{(Equation 9-2)}$$

Now Equation 7-2 gives us the Taylor Series approximation for $\log(1 + i)$:

$$\log(1 + i) = \log(1) + .217(2i - i^2) = .434i - .217i^2$$

For simplicity, let's assume that $.217i^2$ approximately equals 0, so we will ignore it. That means the quantity $\log(1 + i)$ approximately equals $.434i$.

We substitute this into Equation 9-2 above to get:

$$\log(2) = .434ni$$
$$n = .301/.434i = .694/i = 69.4/100i \qquad \text{(Equation 9-3)}$$

where $100i$ is the interest rate expressed as a percent.

Equation 9-3 suggests not the "rule of 72" but the "rule of 69.4" instead. But we must remember that this "rule of 69.4" was obtained by ignoring the term $.217i^2$ in Equation 7-2. If i is large, for example .10, then $.217i^2$ is about .002, which is too big to be ignored. The "rule of 72," even though it too is a linear rule, tends to provide a counterbalance for the squared term.

Table 9-1 below compares the accuracy of the "rule of 72" against the "rule of 69.4."

TABLE 9-1. Estimating the number of years needed to double your money with a constant annual rate of return (i).

i	Rule of 69.4 estimate	Rule of 72 estimate	True Value
.02	34.7	36.0	35.02
.04	17.35	18.0	17.69
.06	11.57	12.0	11.92
.08	8.68	9.0	9.03
.10	6.94	7.2	7.30
.12	5.78	6.0	6.15
.18	3.86	4.0	4.23

The rule of 69.4 is only good when the squared term $(.217i^2)$ is small (i.e., for $i < .06$). The rule of 72 is less accurate for small values of i, but provides an appropriate adjustment for the squared term when i is in the range of .06-.12. As i increases, the rule of 72 begins to lose accuracy, and only becomes good as an approximation.

THE IRA PROBLEM

Suppose you're thirty-two years old when you start an IRA. You deposit $2,000 per year into your IRA until you are sixty-five, for a total of thirty-four deposits. How much money will you have at age sixty-five?

This problem is conceptually more difficult than the compound interest problem, since several deposits are made at different points in time. This problem is sometimes classified mathematically as a uniform series. The formula that we will use is:

$$M = [(1 + i)^n - 1]/i \qquad \text{(Equation 9-4)}$$

The letters M, n, and i have the following definitions:

n = the number of deposits.

M = the multiplier, i.e., your final sum divided by the amount of each deposit.

i = the interest rate computed for the time period associated with each deposit. (A derivation of this formula is given in Appendix D.)

Let's assume that your IRA earns a guaranteed 10% per year, compounded quarterly. But since the formula requires an effective yearly rate of interest (since deposits are made on a yearly basis), we must first compute the effective yearly rate *with compounding.* This will be significantly greater than 10%. The quarterly rate is 2.5%. The effective yearly rate with compounding is obtained by compounding the quarterly rate four times. Mathematically this becomes $(1.025)^4$. Sparing the details, this calculation gives a value of 1.111, which translates to an effective yearly rate of 11.1%.

Now, back to Equation 9-4, where we have i = .111 (yearly interest rate), n = 34 (number of deposits), and M is the object of our calculation. We plug in the numbers to obtain:

$$M = [(1.11)^{34} - 1] / .111$$

Skipping the details, we obtain log(1.11) by Taylor Series as approximately .0477. We multiply this by 34 to get 1.621, and then take the antilog to get $(1.11)^{34}$ as approximately 41.8.

Going back to our formula, we now have:

$$M = (41.8 - 1) / .111, \text{ or } 40.8 / .111 = \text{about } 368.$$

We interpret this value of M as the multiplier of our yearly deposit of $2,000. Thus, after 34 deposits, we have in the account $2,000 × 368 = $736,000.

Did we forget anything? No! No taxes are removed from this accumulating IRA. So this figure is what we will really have.

Okay, but what about inflation? Who knows what inflation patterns will occur over the next thirty-four years?

Let's assume arbitrarily that the interest rate you get on your IRA averages about 3 points higher than inflation. Then, after inflation the equation 9-4 takes the form:

$$M = [(1.03)^{34} - 1] / .03$$

Again, we leave the details for the reader. By performing the identical calculations with these new numbers, we get a multiplier value of 59.6. Thus, in terms of today's dollars, the IRA's worth will be $2,000 × 59.6 = $119,200.

Taxes and Inflation

Let's not end our analysis here. We can ask a meaningful question about taxes. Since taxes are not paid on an accumulating IRA, this type of investment has a definite advantage over the compound interest type of the previous problem. We can ask how much we save by not paying taxes along the way on yearly interest income.

Our yearly rate is 11.1%. Suppose you are in a marginal tax rate of 40%. Thus, if your IRA money was invested through ordinary compound interest, the actual after-tax rate you would realize would be 60% of 11.1%, or 6.66%. We can recompute the value M using this after-tax rate. Thus, we have:

$$M = [(1.0666)^{34} - 1] / .0666$$

Carrying out this calculation, we get a value for M of approximately 119. Thus, if we had to pay taxes along the way, the worth of the IRA at maturity would be only $2,000 \times 119 = \$238,000$.

Further tax-related savings are probably realized, since the IRA contributions are subtracted directly from taxable income. To calculate savings of this sort, we would need to know your tax rate as you are withdrawing your IRA savings. Too much guesswork would be involved to estimate this rate in a meaningful way. We will therefore dispense with this calculation.

Let's go back to the time of maturity of your IRA, when your account contains $736,000. Suppose you withdraw money at a constant rate per month over a fifteen-year period. How much will you get each month?

Let's assume that the money not yet withdrawn from your IRA is earning interest at the rate of 11.1% as before.

This problem is different from the one of the accumulating IRA. Mathematically, what we must find is the amount of each term in a uniform series, whose present value is given. Equation 9-5 below indicates how this is done.

$$M = i/[1 - (1 + i)^{-n}] \qquad \text{(Equation 9-5)}$$

Here n, i, and M have meanings that are consistent with previous use:

M = the multiplier, i.e., what fraction of the initial money would be included in each uniform payment.
n = the number of payments.
i = the interest rate, effective over the time interval corresponding to each payment.

Here we receive one payment per month for a total of fifteen years. Hence, the total number of payments made is $12 \times 15 = 180$, which is our value for n. Since payments are made on a monthly basis, we must recompute i based on a monthly time period.

How do we do this? The yearly rate is 11.1%. The effective monthly rate is the twelfth root of 1.111. We compute this rate by taking the log of 1.111, dividing by 12, and taking the antilog. This gives 1.0088, or an effective monthly rate of 0.88%.

We can now compute the multiplier M in this way:

$$M = .0088 / 1 - (1.0088)^{-180}$$

We proceed in a straightforward way to compute this, leaving the details as another exercise to the reader. The value of M so obtained is .0112.

This number represents the fraction of our IRA value ($736,000) that will be allocated to each of the 180 payments. Each payment then amounts to .0112 × $736,000 = about $8,240 per month.

Well, so what? What will $8,240 be worth in thirty-four years anyway? That's a good question. And we can provide the answer.

Recall that we had estimated the value of the IRA account in present-day dollars to be about $119,200. Now, using our multiplier of .0112 applied to this new figure, we can estimate that the monthly payments would be the equivalent of .0112 × $119,200, or about $2,120 present-day dollars.

LOAN INTEREST — GOOD OR BAD?

As related in Chapter 1, suppose you want to buy a car from a slick, unctuous used car salesman. He offers you a deal in which you borrow $2,000 and pay it back in monthly payments of $160 over a two-year period. What interest rate is he offering you?

This problem is similar to the last IRA problem in the mathematical sense. This is because uniform payments are involved to cover a present amount. The difference is that here we wish to compute the interest rate, not the monthly payments. Nonetheless, Equation 9-5 is a good starting point for working out this intricate problem. So we have:

$$M = i / [1 - (1 + i)^{-n}]$$

We can't really solve this equation for the interest i, because it appears in both the numerator and denominator, and the two terms containing i are not easily combined.

One method of solving the problem is to solve the equation for the "i" that appears in the numerator. This leads us to Equation 9-6:

$$i = M(1 - (1 + i)^{-n})$$ (Equation 9-6)

It might not look like we've made any progress, but in fact we now have a method for computing i, though it may be repetitive. This works as follows:

1. Take an initial guess at the value of i.
2. Plug the current value of i into the right side of Equation 9-6; evaluate the expression to give a new value of i (since i equals the entire right side).
3. If the previous two values of i so computed are sufficiently close, stop; you've found a good estimate for i.
4. Otherwise, take the newly computed value of i and go back to step 2.

Let's apply this repetitive procedure to our Used Car Salesman problem. Here, the value of M is determined as the ratio of the payments to the amount borrowed, or $160/2,000 = .08$.

Since the payments are to be made monthly over a two-year period, there are twenty-four payments in all, so $n = 24$. The interest rate that is pertinent to Equation 9-6 is then an effective monthly rate. Now let's start with the algorithm.

Step 1. For an initial guess of i, let's pick 1.5%. This is equivalent to an 18% annual rate.

Step 2. We are to evaluate the right side of Equation 9-6, using $M = .08$ and $i = .015$. We must start with the "hard part" by computing $(1.015)^{-24}$.

First, we estimate $\log(1.015)$ by Taylor Series to obtain .00651 ($= .434 \times .015$). Now multiply this by -24. This gives $-.156$. Now take the antilog; mindful that the characteristic is 1 and the mantissa is .844, we get the antilog estimate as .699. Continuing to evaluate the right side of Equation 9-6, we now have $.08(1 - .699) = .024$. This is the computed value of i.

Since this differs significantly from our last value of i (.015), we need to perform a second calculation. So we take this new value of i, plug it into the right side of Equation 9-6, and evaluate:

$$i = M(1 - (1.024)^{-24})$$

This calculation gives a value for i of .035. Since this again differs significantly from .024, we proceed again, plugging .035 into the right side of Equation 9-6.

Continuing in this extremely laborious procedure, we obtain successive estimates of .044, .052, .059, and .060, at which point we can call it quits, since the last two estimates are acceptably close.

This tells us that our loan is at a monthly rate of 6.0%, or at a yearly rate of (gasp!) 72%. Is this right? Believe it or not, yes! A check of the interest rate tables shows that, indeed, this is the rate that the Used Car Salesman is trying to push off on us.

We should be asking a question right now. Why was this so much work? We had to compute a difficult expression for values of .015, .024, .035, .044, .052, .059, and .060, or seven times in all.

The answer, in part, is that our initial guess was extremely bad. When we guessed that the yearly rate might be about 18%, we were sadly naive to the scheming trickery of the used car salesman.

We might have made a more intelligent initial guess by noting that our total payments come to $160 × 24 = $3,840. This is approximately 95% more than our actual loan of $2,000. A better initial guess would be obtained by using this 95%, and taking into account that the loan is over two years. Thus, we might roughly estimate the effective rate at about 47.5%. If we had made this initial guess, we would have "converged" in only three steps.

In problems of a more realistic nature, where shady used car salesmen don't throw things too out of proportion, our chances of making a good initial guess are much better. Then this method becomes quite workable in terms of effort required.

HOUSE PAYMENTS

Suppose you want to buy a house for $100,000, and are planning a down payment of 20%, or $20,000. You will then borrow the remainder, $80,000 at a rate of 12% yearly. You will make constant monthly payments over a thirty-year period. What will your monthly payments be?

In the housing financing world, there is a familiar rule-of-thumb that your monthly payments are approximately equal to the amount borrowed divided by 100. Using this rule, we would obtain an estimate of $800 as a monthly payment, which is a very good estimate. But let's check this mathematically.

As you might have guessed, Equation 9-5 is to be used here. Since we are to make twelve payments a year for a total of thirty years, we choose n = 12 × 30 = 360. For i, we choose the equivalent monthly rate of 12% yearly, or .01. Equation 9-5 now takes the following form:

$$M = .01 \; / \; [1 - (1.01)^{-360}]$$

Let's start with the calculation $(1.01)^{-360}$. The log of 1.01 can be quickly approximated as .434(.01) = .0043. Now multiply this by −360 to obtain −1.55. The antilog is 2.82×10^{-2}, or .028, which is our estimate for $(1.01)^{-360}$.

The problem now becomes M = .01/.972, or about .0103.

This fraction represents the amount of each payment divided by the total amount borrowed. We see it is very close to one in one hundred as our approximation method told us.

In fact, the calculation of $(1 + i)^{-n}$ is very close to 0 when n is a large number such as 360.

With this reasoning, we come up with a rule for approximating monthly house payments. Divide the yearly mortgage rate by 12 to obtain the effective monthly rate. This will be an approximation for the multiplier M. Then multiply this value of M by the amount borrowed to approximate monthly payments. (Actually, your payments may be slightly higher because of closing costs, taxes, and other fees.)

What about your tax benefit? This is difficult to estimate over the entire length of your mortgage, since your interest payments continually change. Initially, almost all your payments will be interest payments, and therefore tax deductible. If your marginal tax rate is 40%, then your actual after-tax payments will be about 60% of $800 (as in our example), or about $488.

CHOOSING THE BETTER INVESTMENT

Suppose you have a cash fund of $10,000 that you would like to invest. Two investment opportunities present themselves, of which you can choose only one.

Under plan A, you invest the entire $10,000 at once. Your return is $1,000 per year for thirteen years.

Under plan B, you invest $4,000 and get a return of $1,100 per year for four years.

Which plan is preferable? Assume that any funds not currently tied up are able to gain interest at 10% yearly.

First, we must determine a method of comparing these two plans mathematically. One way is to take the longer of the two time periods, in this case thirteen years, and compute the money that will be available by both plans in that time period. That calculation is burdensome, as you can see if you try it.

A second way is to compute the effective interest rate that each plan offers. This should remind you somewhat of the difficulty we had in solving the Used Car Salesman Problem. The situation here is even more complicated, since funds are invested at different rates over varying time periods.

The third method, the preferred one, is to compute everything in terms of the present value. This method is the most straightforward and logical, and it is also the most feasible mathematically.

To apply this method, there are two new formulas we need to be aware of. The first, Equation 9-7, gives the present value of a single sum of money transacted at some future time.

$$M = (1 + i)^{-n} \qquad \text{(Equation 9-7)}$$

Here, M is the multiplier, i.e, the ratio of the money's present worth to its future worth; i is the rate of interest per period; and n is the number of periods in the future at which the money is transacted.

Equation 9-8 gives the present value of a uniform series.

$$M = [1 - (1 + i)^{-n}] / i \qquad \text{(Equation 9-8)}$$

Here again, M is the multiplier, i.e., the ratio between present worth and the value of each future installment; i is the interest rate effective for the period corresponding to each installment; and n is the number of installments.

We can use Equation 9-7 to evaluate the present value of the cash flows presented through plans A and B.

Considering plan A first, we have a uniform series of $1,000 per year for thirteen years. We have i = .10 and n = 13. Plugging the numbers in:

$$M = [1 - (1.10)^{-13}] / .10$$

Leaving the details to the reader, we obtain here a value of M of approximately 7.07. Thus, the present value of this series is $7,070.

Now looking at plan B, we have a similar uniform series, namely a return of $1,100 per year for four years. Here we apply Equation

9-7 with n = 4 and i = .10. Leaving the details to the reader, we obtain a value of M of 3.16. This value multiplied by the value of each installment ($1,100) gives the present value of the series as approximately $3,480.

Plan B also has an un-invested $6,000, which we add to $3,460 to obtain $9,480 as the total present value of plan B.

Finally, since the present value of plan B exceeds that of plan A, we conclude that plan B provides the better investment under these circumstances.

With that, we'll close out our discussion of interest rate problems. This class is among the most interesting as well as the most difficult of problems that you are likely to face in day-to-day living.

Chapter 10

Trig Functions

The ability to estimate trigonometric functions in your head, or at least without the aid of a machine, can be immensely rewarding. Such skill opens whole new vistas of problems, which suddenly become doable.

Many people associate the word "trigonometry" only with triangles. Trigonometry does deal with triangles, but it is also much more. Many applications from physics require the use of trig functions to solve. Innumerable problems of geometry, which have no apparent connection to triangles, involve trig functions in their solutions. And there are infinitely more applications from such unlikely areas as electrical engineering, quantum mechanics, astronomy, and mechanical vibrations.

Obviously, we don't have the room to discuss all of these applications, but we will do some examples from the more interesting areas. You will soon discover that developing a facility with trig functions can greatly enhance your enjoyment of machine-free mathematics.

In this chapter, we'll review the basic theory behind trig functions and then discuss the methods for estimating them. In later chapters, we'll get involved in some exciting applications.

So, let's start off here with some basic theory.

UNIT CIRCLE

The first point that's noteworthy about the trig functions is that they are actually defined in terms of a circle, rather than in terms of a triangle. So to begin, examine the circle of Figure 10-1. This circle has its center at the origin of a coordinate system and a radius of 1. Such a circle is called a unit circle. One radius (necessarily of length 1) is drawn. Its angle, measured from the positive x-axis in a counter-clockwise direction, is denoted as Θ (Greek letter theta).

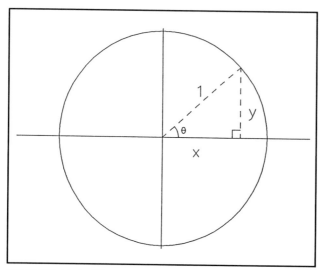

FIGURE 10-1. *The unit circle.*

The radius intersects the circle's edge at some point (x,y). We define the six trigonometric functions of Θ in terms of the values of x and y:

TABLE 10-1. Basic trigonometric functions.

Trig Function	Abbreviation	Definition
sine Θ	sin Θ	y
cosine Θ	cos Θ	x
tangent Θ	tan Θ	y/x
cotangent Θ	cot Θ	x/y
secant Θ	sec Θ	1/x
cosecant Θ	csc Θ	1/y

The unit circle is a concept that is so basic to trigonometry that we will spend some time discussing it.

First, notice that the angle Θ can take on any value whatsoever. The values of the functions vary in accordance with changes in Θ. Table 10-2 indicates how the trig functions change along with the angle Θ.

TABLE 10-2. Trig function ranges for various Θ ranges.

Trig Function	Range of Θ (degrees)			
	0° to 90°	90° to 180°	180° to 270°	270° to 360°
sin Θ	0 to 1	1 to 0	0 to -1	-1 to 0
cos Θ	1 to 0	0 to -1	-1 to 0	0 to 1
tan Θ	0 to inf.	-inf. to 0	0 to inf.	-inf. to 0
cot Θ	inf. to 0	0 to -inf.	inf. to 0	0 to -inf.
sec Θ	1 to inf.	-inf. to -1	-1 to -inf.	inf. to 1
csc Θ	inf. to 1	1 to inf.	-inf. to -1	-1 to -inf.

(inf. = an indefinitely large number)

In practice, the most commonly used functions are sin and cos. From now on in this book, we will use only sin, cos, and tan. Notice that all other trig functions can be expressed in terms of sin and cos in this way:

$$\tan(\Theta) = \sin(\Theta)/\cos(\Theta)$$
$$\cot(\Theta) = \cos(\Theta)/\sin(\Theta)$$
$$\sec(\Theta) = 1/\cos(\Theta)$$
$$\csc(\Theta) = 1/\sin(\Theta)$$

Next, note in Figure 10-1 that a right triangle can be formed by dropping a perpendicular line from a point (x,y) to the x-axis. The right triangle obtained has sides of x and y and a hypotenuse of 1. This gives us the first trigonometric identity. Since $\sin(\Theta) = y$ and $\cos(\Theta) = x$, from the Pythagorean Theorem we have $\sin^2(\Theta) + \cos^2(\Theta) = 1$ for all values of Θ.

TRIANGLES

On that thought, let's part with our unit circle for the time being and turn our attention to triangles. Remember the method of forming triangles from the unit circle, by dropping a perpendicular from the point (x,y) onto the positive axis. In this way, two very important triangles can be formed.

The two triangles are termed, because of their angle values, as the 30-60-90 triangle and the 45-45-90 triangle. Figure 10-2 shows the 30-60-90 triangle along with the lengths of its sides.

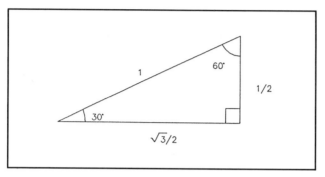

FIGURE 10-2. *The 30–60–90 triangle.*

Keeping in mind the definitions of the trig functions, we can see the following from Figure 10-2:

$\sin(30°) = \frac{1}{2}$
$\cos(30°) = \sqrt{3}/2 = $ about .866
$\tan(30°) = [\frac{1}{2}] / [\sqrt{3} / 2] = \sqrt{3}/3 = $ about .577

What may not be quite so obvious is that we can "flip" the triangle on its side so that the 60° angle corresponds to Θ in the unit circle of Figure 10-1. Then we can apply the trig function definitions to obtain:

$\sin(60°) = \sqrt{3}/2 = $ about .866
$\cos(60°) = \frac{1}{2}$
$\tan(60°) = [\sqrt{3} / 2] / \frac{1}{2} = \sqrt{3} = $ about 1.732

A more subtle observation can be made by comparing the sines and cosines of 30° and 60°. You may have noticed that $\sin(30°) = \cos(60°)$ and $\sin(60°) = \cos(30°)$. In general, it is true that $\cos(\Theta) = \sin(90° - \Theta)$, and similarly that $\sin(\Theta) = \cos(90° - \Theta)$. Interestingly, these relations hold for all values of Θ, even those outside of the range of 0° to 90°.

Figure 10-3 shows the 45-45-90 triangle along with its lengths. By examination of this triangle, we see that:

$\sin(45°) = \sqrt{2}/2 = $ about .707
$\cos(45°) = \sqrt{2}/2 = $ about .707
$\tan(45°) = 1$

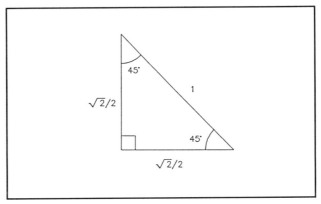

FIGURE 10-3. *The 45–45–90 triangle.*

So far, we know the sines, cosines, and tangents of 30°, 60°, and 45°. This is a good start, but it really isn't enough on which to base an estimation scheme. I would suggest that you become familiar with four more values as follows:

$\sin(10°) = .174$
$\sin(20°) = .342$
$\sin(70°) = .940$
$\sin(80°) = .985$

Actually, $\sin(70°)$ and $\sin(80°)$ could have been deducted from $\sin(20°)$ and $\sin(10°)$ respectively (since, e.g., $\sin(70°) = \cos(20°)$ and $\cos(20°) = \sqrt{[1 - \sin^2(20°)]}$). But a little extra remembering is probably worth the trouble here.

Using the above four values, we can compute the corresponding cosines quite easily, since $\cos(\Theta) = \sin(90° - \Theta)$. Then we can compute the tangents as the ratios of sines to cosines. Once we have done this, we can summarize our knowledge of trig function values in Table 10-3.

Depending on how good you are at division, you may or may not want to try memorizing the tangent values. Personally, I prefer to remember them instead of dividing sin/cos whenever I need one of them. But it's a matter of personal taste.

ESTIMATING TRIG FUNCTIONS

Now you're ready to estimate all the values of these trig functions. How do you do it? My suggestion is linear interpolation between

TABLE 10-3. Summary of trig function values.

Θ (degrees)	sin Θ	cos Θ	tan Θ
0°	0	1	0
10°	.174	.985	.176
20°	.342	.940	.364
30°	.500	.866	.577
45°	.707	.707	1.000
60°	.866	.500	1.732
70°	.940	.342	2.748
80°	.985	.174	5.671
90°	1	0	inf.

two known values. Since you know the values of several of the trig functions, you are prepared to do this with acceptable accuracy. This would not be acceptable for estimating the higher tangent function values, however. Here I would suggest the laborious but more accurate procedure of estimating the sine, then estimating the cosine, and finally dividing the sine by the cosine. You will see this in an example later.

But before doing some estimation examples, we'll pause to discuss one more point of theory necessary in estimating by Taylor Series.

Refer to the unit circle of Figure 10-1. Here, Θ was measured in terms of degrees. This is a very arbitrary unit of measure, since it depends on an arbitrary concept of dividing a circle into 360° (why this number?). A more natural unit of measurement, at least mathematically, is the radian.

The radian is actually just a length of a radius (1 in the case of the unit circle) measured along the circle's circumference. Since the circumference of a circle is equal to 2π times the radius, this means that there are 2π radians in the circle's circumference. Thus, there is a simple relationship between radians and degrees. There are $360/2\pi$ degrees in one radian, or about 57.3°. Similarly, there are $1/57.3$ or about .0175 radians in 1°.

All of this is only of interest to us when we are taking the derivatives of the trig functions for use in Taylor Series approximations. If the angle Θ is measured in radians, then the derivative of sin(Θ) is cos(Θ); and the derivative of cos(Θ) is –sin(Θ). If Θ is measured in degrees, then the derivative of sin(Θ) is .0175 cos(Θ), and the derivative of cos(Θ) is –.0175 sin(Θ) (since $1° = .0175$ radians).

The second derivatives of these trig functions involve the square of .0175 and are therefore small. A small second derivative is, incidentally, a good indication that linear interpolation works well, as, in fact, it does with the trig functions using our set of values in Table 10-3. It works well enough so that no jack-ups or jack-downs are necessary to obtain two decimal points of accuracy.

When extreme accuracy is required, however, the Taylor Series approximations of equations 10-1 and 10-2 below may be used:

$$\sin(x + y) = \sin(x) + .0175 \cos(x)y - .00015 \sin(x)y^2$$
(Equation 10-1)

$$\cos(x + y) = \cos(x) - .0175 \sin(x)y - .00015 \cos(x)y^2$$
(Equation 10-2)

Taylor Series has limited practical usage for trig function problems, however, since linear interpolation is normally an excellent approximator. Taylor Series is of some interest when estimating the trigonometric functions of very small angles (i.e., when cos(x) is approximately 1 and y^2 can be neglected in Equation 10-1). Here, Equation 10-1 reduces to:

$$\sin(x) = .0175 \ x, \text{ for x in degrees} \qquad \text{(Equation 10-3)}$$

This equation is useful in many problems, though it is not always precise. The approximation is good when x is small, but as x grows larger, the approximation grows worse.

An Example

Presumably the reader remembers well the method of linear interpolation from the chapter on logarithms. One quick example may be in order here, however.

Let's compute sin(63°) by linear interpolation. We will compute this as three-tenths of the way between .866 and .940 (sin(60°) and sin(70°) respectively), or .866 + .3(.074), which, when the dust clears, is .888. The actual tabled value is .891.

Now suppose it is really tan(63°) that we wish to know. Since the tangent function changes extremely rapidly (with a high second derivative) for values greater than 45°, it would be unwise to compute tan(63°) by linear interpolation.

But we do know sin(63°) (estimated as .888), and we can estimate cos(63°) by an identical method. Thus, we can estimate cos(63°) as seven-tenths of the way from cos(70°) (.342) to cos(60°) (.500). This works out to about .455.

Now, we can put it all together. The tangent will be sin divided by the cosine, or .888/.455. We carry out this division for our estimate of tan(63°) to be approximately 1.951. This compares with the actual tabled value of 1.962. So we didn't do too badly.

Before passing on to the next topic, we should mention angles greater than 90°. A previous pair of relationships tells us that $\sin(\Theta) = \cos(90° - \Theta)$, and $\cos(\Theta) = (90° - \Theta)$. These relationships hold for all values of Θ, even those greater than 90°.

Just for fun, let's compute sin(120°). We are told that this is equal to $\cos(90° - 120°) = \cos(-30°)$. To compute cos(−30°), check the unit circle of Figure 10-1, and you will see that $\cos(-\Theta) = \cos(\Theta)$, mindful of the definition of the cosine function as the x-coordinate along the circle. So we have $\sin(120°) = \cos(30°) = .866$.

If we want to compute cos(135°), we use $\sin(90° - 135°) = \sin(-45°)$, but then we should consult the unit circle to see that $\sin(-\Theta) = -\sin(\Theta)$. This is again in keeping with the definition of the sine function as the y-coordinate. So, our estimate for cos(135°) is −.707. Computing trig functions for angles outside of the range of 0° to 90° will be important in analyzing oblique triangles, i.e., triangles in which one of the angles exceeds 90°.

INVERSE TRIG FUNCTIONS

As you may have guessed, we also have to deal with inverse trig functions. Some problems may require us to compute an angle given a trig function value. The notation for this inverse function that we will use in this book is the prefix "arc." By arcsin(x), we will mean the angle whose sine is x. Similarly defined will be arccos(x) and arctan(x).

Again, the most practical way of computing the inverse functions is by linear interpolation. For example, to compute arcsin(.300), we would note that arcsin(.176) = 10°, and arcsin(.364) = 20°. Therefore, we would estimate arcsin(.300) as the fraction (.300 − .176)/(.364 − .176) of the way between 10° and 20°.

The fraction works out to .124/.188. We can see that this is just a bit less than 2/3, so we may quickly guess this fraction decimally as .65. The required angle would therefore be about 16.5°, or 16° 30′.

In this book, we will not discuss the Taylor Series approximations for the inverse trig functions. The derivatives of these functions are extremely laborious to compute, and the extra accuracy obtained is simply not worth the effort.

I should mention something that many readers may already have caught. In the example of finding the angle whose sine is .300, 16.5° is not the only answer. 163.5° is another answer (refer to the unit circle to check this) and, if you really want to get technical, 376.5° is an answer and so is –345.5°. In fact, there are an infinity of angles whose sine is .300.

In theoretical mathematics, this problem is avoided by defining the arcsin function as limited to the range from -90° to 90°. In this way, all values that arcsin can have are taken on once and only once. In practice, the problem of multiple solutions to the inverse trig functions should not stir you.

SOME PRACTICE

So far, we've been talking about a lot of theory and not much practical application. It will do us good to try one simple example right now.

You are to row a boat across a river. You are capable of rowing the boat at a speed of 7 miles per hour (you're a fairly good rower). The river current is 2 miles per hour from left to right. At what angle should you steer your boat so as to arrive at the other side at a point directly across from your starting position?

This problem is an example of force vectors. There are two forces acting on the boat — the force that you exert and the force that the current exerts. Forces are "vectors," which means they have the properties of magnitude and direction.

Both the magnitude and the direction of the force created by the river current are known. The magnitude of the force created by you is known. The direction is to be determined.

The situation can be represented in a diagram such as Figure 10-4. Here the vectors are drawn as arrows. The directions of the arrows correspond with the directions of the forces, and the lengths of the arrows correspond to the magnitudes of the forces.

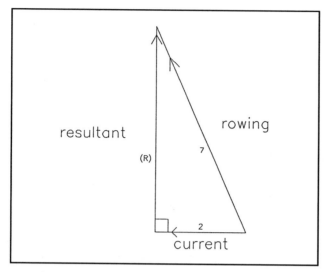

FIGURE 10-4. *Force vector representation of the problem of crossing a river.*

In the diagram, we want the resultant vector R to point in a direction directly across the river. This situation leaves us with a right triangle, as indicated. Our theory developed so far is directly applicable. The only notable difference is that here the hypotenuse is not 1, as in the case of the unit circle, but 7. Then sin(Θ) is equal to 2/7 from the diagram. (Generally, the sine is the ratio of the angle's opposite side to the triangle's hypotenuse, when dealing with right triangles). Similarly, the cosine is the ratio of the angle's adjacent side to the hypotenuse, and the tangent is the ratio of the opposite side to the adjacent side. All this is consistent with the theory developed for unit circles.

The solution to the problem is the value of Θ, which is determined as arcsin(2/7), or arcsin(.286).

This angle is determined by linear interpolation, using the facts that arcsin(.174) = 10° and arcsin(.342) = 20°. Leaving the details as an exercise to the reader, we obtain the value of Θ to be approximately 16.7°.

This example typifies the use of trig functions in solving right triangles. Since the right triangle concept is closely linked to the unit circle, the use of the trig functions here is easily comprehensible. What is not so obvious is the use of trig functions to solve triangles (by "solving triangles" we mean calculating the lengths of its unknown sides and the values of its unknown angles) that are not right triangles.

OTHER TRIANGLES

It seems that the world is full of right triangles, and it is rare that we have to worry about other types. Yet they do exist in profusion. To help you solve these triangles, I will present two trigonometric equations without proof. Equation 10-4 is called the Law of Sines and Equation 10-5 is called the Law of Cosines.

$a/\sin(A) = b/\sin(B) = c/\sin(C)$ (Equation 10-4) Law of Sines
$a^2 = b^2 + c^2 - (2bc)\cos(A)$ (Equation 10-5) Law of Cosines

In these two equations, A, B, and C refer to the respective angles of the triangle, and a, b, and c refer to the lengths of the sides opposite to angles A, B, and C respectively.

Notice that the Law of Cosines reduces to just the Pythagorean Theorem if $A = 90°$, and therefore $\cos(A) = 0$.

As an example where these methods are used, let's compute the three angles of a triangle of unknown shape whose sides are of lengths 15, 11, and 8.

First, we note that in fact this is a valid triangle, since no one side has a length greater than the sum of the lengths of the other two sides. Next, we note that the triangle does not have a right angle, since 15^2 does not equal $11^2 + 8^2$. The fact that 15^2 is greater than $11^2 + 8^2$ should suggest to us that the largest angle (i.e., the angle opposite the longest side) is greater than $90°$.

We could conceivably start out using the Law of Sines. This should give us a proportional relationship between the angles; we would then use the fact that the angles sum to $180°$ to compute the three individual values.

But this is so hard! It would be much easier to use the Law of Cosines first, to deduce the value of one angle, and then apply the Law of Sines. This is how we will proceed.

Let's label the sides a = 15, b = 11, and c = 8, in decreasing order of length and alphabet. Applying the Law of Cosines, we have:

$225 = 121 + 64 - 2(11)(8)\cos(A)$
$225 = 185 - 176\cos(A)$
$\cos(A) = -40/176 = -.227$

Now, we are to compute arccos(-.227). Surprise! We have a negative cosine value! And none of the values that we learned in Table 4 are negative. What are we to do?

Well, we have to go back to basics, as usual, and look at the unit circle of Figure 10-1. Keeping in mind the perfect symmetry of this circle, and also the definition of the cosine, can you see that $\cos(180° - \Theta) = -\cos(\Theta)$? We shall use this relationship. First, we will compute arccos(.227), and then subtract this value from 180 to obtain arccos(-.227).

We know that arccos(.174) = 80°, and that arccos(.342) = 70°. Estimate arccos(.227) by linear interpolation as approximately 76.8°. We then estimate arccos(-.227) as 103.2°.

Now to the Law of Sines to complete the problem. First, we will write:

$a/\sin(A) = b/\sin(B)$; or
$15/\sin(103.2°) = 11/\sin(B)$

Everything is known except the angle B, but first we must compute sin(103.2°). I'll leave it as an exercise for the reader to see that $\sin(180 - \Theta) = \sin(\Theta)$. So, $\sin(103.2°) = \sin(76.8°)$. By linear interpolation, we can estimate sin(76.8°) as about .971. This gives us:

$15/.971 = 11/\sin(B)$
$\sin(B) = (.971)(11)/15 = $ about .713.

Now we find the angle B as arcsin(.713). Use linear interpolation with arcsin(.707) = 45° and arcsin(.866) = 60°. This gives us an approximation for the angle B as 45.6°.

Angle C is then found by using the fact that the sum of the three angles is 180°. Since angle A is 103.2° and angle B is 45.6°, this leaves 31.2° for angle C. As a check, make sure that the largest angle is opposite the longest side, and the smallest angle is opposite the smallest side.

This chapter has been mainly theoretical and has laid the groundwork for the more interesting problems that will come in the following chapters. I think you will be amazed by the fascinating array of problems that you can solve once you are armed with the facility of dealing with trig functions. Some of these problems you will probably find useful, and others you may not. But, if you are like me, you will find all of them fun.

Chapter 11

A Protractor, A Ruler, and Gray Matter

After having sifted through a whole chapter of theory, it's time now to start working out some problems. I find trig functions to be entertaining and exciting even more than they are directly useful.

Trig functions enable you to work on problems that occur in the natural world. As mentioned in the introduction of the previous chapter, the applications of trig functions among the natural sciences are wide and varied. If you are personally involved in such an area, you are assuredly well-versed in these applications.

FUN APPLICATIONS OF TRIG FUNCTIONS

As for the layman rather than the scientific specialist, trig functions provide a means to explore the world with a keener eye. When I go hiking in the mountains, I take immense enjoyment in bringing along a protractor and a small pocket ruler. I might be interested in estimating the height of a prominent tree on a distant slope, the elevation of a certain peak, the distance across a lake, or the distances to various points viewed from atop a mountain peak or ridge.

Such problems may not seem crucial to some people, but if you enjoy machine-free math, they can provide you with a good deal of satisfaction and fascination.

TRIANGULATION

The most basic concept in these types of problems is called triangulation. Triangulation really means deducing the location of a distant object based on two separate sightings.

This is the basic idea behind locating aircraft through radio signals received at two different stations. In astronomy, it is one method used to determine the distances to stars. It is based on the idea that the Earth occupies different points in the heavens during different times of the year. Thus, the sightings of the stars should vary accordingly, and their distances can then be trigonometrically deduced.

I once remarked to a friend of mine that I use this method in the mountains to calculate distances to certain locations. My pseudo-intellectual companion, doubtlessly thinking about taking sightings while climbing up and down, remarked, "Yes, but the three points involved have to lie in the same plane."

To this I answered, "Three points define a plane," and the discussion was quickly put to rest. This is an important point. You don't have to consider the approximately flat surface of the Earth as being the only possible realm on which to form a triangle for your purposes. Any three points define a single plane; this plane may be difficult to conceptualize physically at times, yet it does exist.

When measuring angles with a protractor, the plane of your triangle has to be kept in mind. When measuring an angle, your protractor should always be aligned with the plane of your triangle.

The theory behind triangulation is shown in Figure 11-1.

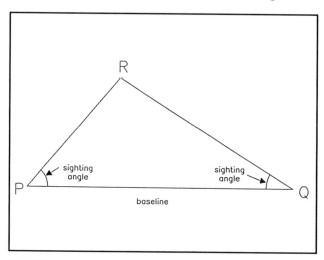

FIGURE 11-1. *The method of triangulation.*

In Figure 11-1, the location of point R is desired. Sightings are taken from points P and Q. Thus, the angles RPQ (the angle between R and Q measured at P) and RQP are measured. In measuring these angles, it is important to keep your protractor in the plane defined by the three points R, P, and Q.

In Figure 11-1 the distance PQ is termed the "baseline" and is assumed to be known. If you are hiking in the mountains or engaging in some such activity, you may not know this distance. But take heart. You can measure it if you know the length of your foot. You can simply step it off, placing one foot carefully in front of and adjoining the previous one. Make sure that your distance is a straight line distance, or a reasonable approximation to one. If you are walking a winding trail while trying to measure a baseline distance, don't expect an accurate result to your triangulation.

Solving the triangle RPQ is not difficult. Since angles RPQ and RQP are known, the third angle is determined by simple subtraction from 180°. Then the Law of Sines can be used to determine the lengths of the other two sides. In general, the longer the baseline, the more accurate your answer will be.

DISTANCE ACROSS A LAKE

Okay, it's time for an example. Suppose you are considering swimming across a wilderness lake of unknown size. If you don't make it, no one will be around to save you. So, it seems reasonable that you want to estimate the distance that you will be swimming. You spot a tree on the other side of the lake, which you use as point R. Then you take sightings from P and Q and measure the baseline. You obtain the following measurements:

Angle RPQ = 80°
Angle RQP = 75°
Distance PQ = 400 feet

First, we know at once the third angle of the triangle (angle R) as 180-80-75 degrees, or 25°. Now we can estimate the distance PR as follows, using the Law of Sines:

$PR/(\sin(75°)) = 400 / (\sin(25°))$
or $PR = [400(\sin(75°))] / (\sin(25°))$

The two sines can be estimated by linear interpolation. Sin(75°) is approximately midway between .940 and .985 (.963), and sin(25°) is approximately midway between .342 and .500 (.421). So we have:

$PR = 400(.963) / (.421) = 385.2 / .421$

We can perform this division by conventional means to obtain an approximate distance of 920 feet.

Triangulation becomes an extremely simple procedure if one of the angles of the triangle is 90°. Usually, this can be arranged by orientation of the baseline.

Suppose we are estimating the distance across a second lake by the same method, except this time we set things up in such a way that the angle RQP is 90°. In other words, we pace off our baseline at right angles to our sighting of the tree on the other side.

After pacing off 100 feet to point P, we take a second sighting and observe the angle RPQ as 86°. The situation is diagrammed in Figure 11-2.

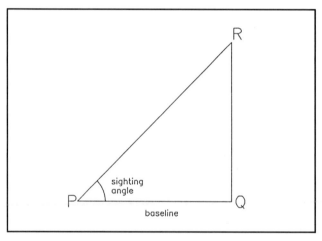

FIGURE 11-2. *Triangulation with right-angled baseline.*

Here, the calculation of the distance QR is computed as PQtan(P), or just 100tan(86°).

The tangent of 86° is best computed as the ratio of sin(86°)/cos(86°). Each of these can be estimated by linear interpolation. Sin(86°) is approximately six-tenths of the way from .985 to 1(.994), and cos(86°) is approximately four-tenths of the way from 0 to .174 (.070). The tangent, then, is the ratio .994/.070, or after dividing, about 14.20. The distance across the lake is then approximated at 14.20(100 feet), or 1,420 feet.

ESTIMATING HEIGHTS

A second kind of interesting problem is estimating the height of a distant object. In the mountains, I enjoy calculating the heights of surrounding peaks by this method. The idea is to take two sightings of the peak, measuring the angle to the horizontal (also called the angle of elevation) at each point. The points should be chosen colinear, or "in line with" the peak. The situation is diagrammed in Figure 11-3.

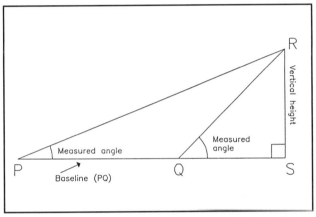

FIGURE 11-3. *Procedure for estimating the height of a distant object.*

Here, the following measurement procedure is used:

1. From point P, measure the angle RPQ, which is really just the angle of elevation of the peak R.
2. Walk off a measured distance toward the peak while maintaining the same elevation. Call this distance PQ.
3. From this point Q, measure the angle RQS, which is actually just a second angle of elevation of the peak R.

Now, how do we analyze this situation? In Figure 11-3, consider first triangle PQR. In this triangle, we know the angle RQP and the distance PQ, both by direct measurement. We can also deduce the value of the angle PQR since it is the supplement of angle RQS, which we know. Specifically, angle PQR is 180° minus angle RQS. We now know two angles of the triangle RPQ, which means that we can easily compute the third. Using the Law of Sines, we can compute the length QR.

Next, we can look at triangle RQS. We know that this is a right triangle (since the vertical direction is always perpendicular to the horizontal direction). We know the angle RQS by measurement, and we know the distance QR by our previous calculations. So we have enough information to solve for the distance RS, which is our desired height. Note that this height is the elevation above our current height, not the elevation above sea level.

This problem is more difficult than ordinary triangulation. This is because calculations must be performed on two separate triangles. Let's illustrate with an example.

Suppose you observe the angle of elevation of a peak to be 15° from a point P on the horizontal. You step off 1,000 feet toward the peak (presumably you have a consistent walking stride that you have measured). From this new point, you measure a second angle of elevation as 22°. How high is the peak?

Referring to Figure 11-3, we have:

angle RPQ = 15°
angle RQS = 22°
angle PQR = 180° − 22° = 158°
distance PQ = 1,000 feet
angle PRQ = 180° − 158° − 15° = 7°

Armed with these figures, we can now compute the distance QR as follows, using the Law of Sines:

(QR) / (sin(15°)) = (PQ) / (sin(7°))
or QR = [1,000(sin(15°))] / (sin(7°))

The sine values are computed by linear interpolation. Sin(15°) is approximately midway between .174 and .342 (.258). Sin(7°) is about seven-tenths of .174 (.122). Thus, we have:

QR = (1,000)(.258) / (.122) = 258 / .122 = about 2,115.

Now, knowing the hypotenuse QR and the angle RQS of the right triangle RQS, we can compute the vertical height RS as QRsin (RQS), or 2,115 (sin(22°)).

The sine of 22 is about two-tenths of the way from .174 to .342, or about .208. The desired height is the product (2,115)(.208) — approximately 440 feet. This does not represent the height of the peak above sea level. It represents the height of the peak over your level.

More Complex Problems

More complex variations of this problem are possible, if you are limited by geographical terrain features. Thus, if you cannot step off the distance PQ in a direction toward the peak or along the horizontal, you can draw a new diagram similar to Figure 11-3, and reformulate the problem.

Unfortunately, the new formulation may require three-dimensional artistry on your part. The two triangles of Figure 11-3 were in the same plane, due to the care that we took in constructing them. But, if the two triangles were in different planes, we would find ourselves with a problem of three dimensions, still quite doable, but difficult to conceptualize graphically.

Another problem exists if, referring to Figure 11-3, you do not traverse the distance PQ along level ground. In this case, you must be able to estimate somehow the amount of your vertical increase in elevation between points P and Q. In practice, this could be tricky, if not impossible, to perform accurately. My suggestion is that, for problems of this type, you stay to the method of Figure 11-3.

ESTIMATING DISTANCES

One problem that is particularly enjoyable to me is that of estimating distances to certain places while atop a mountain peak. This problem, as far as the trigonometry is concerned, is not difficult, but it is necessary to know the height of the mountain above the surrounding tableland. If this information is not easily obtainable from maps, then the method described in the previous example can be used before the mountain is ascended. The trigonometric representation of this problem is depicted in Figure 11-4.

In Figure 11-4, only the angle P needs to be measured. The distance PQ is assumed known, since you might know the elevation of the mountain less the elevation of the surrounding land. You also can assume that the angle Q is a right angle.

The horizontal distance to the point R is then just the distance QR, which is computed as PRtan(P).

By way of an example, suppose you are at the top of a mountain whose elevation you know to be 6,400 feet. You also know the elevation of a town near the base of the mountain to be 2,500 feet. So the distance PQ is then the difference 6,400 – 2,500 = 3,900 feet.

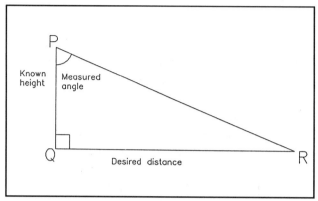

FIGURE 11-4. *Estimating the distance to a certain point from an elevated position.*

Now you take a sighting of a distant object that is approximately at the same elevation as the base of the mountain (this is important!), and obtain a value of 22° for the angle P. What is the distance of this object?

Referring to Figure 11-4, we need the distance QR = PRtan(P), or 3,900tan(22°). So, to start, we need to estimate the tangent of 22%. If you know the tangent values, all you need do is linear interpolation between tan(20°) and tan(30°).

I'll assume that you don't know these tangent values. Then, hang with me and we'll compute tan(22°) as the ratio sin(22°) / cos(22°).

Sin(22°) is approximately two-tenths of the way from .342 to .500, or about .374. Cos(22°) is approximately eight-tenths of the way from .866 to .940, or about .925. Our tangent estimation then is .374/.925. This works out to just about .400.

Finally, then, our distance is calculated as 3,900 × .400 = 1,560 feet.

ESTIMATING SIZES

Suppose that we wish to estimate the size of an object so sighted in the distance. The dimensions of such an object can be found quite readily once the distance of the object is known.

The method that can be used for solving this kind of problem is based on the geometric principle of similar triangles. According to this rule, triangles are said to be similar if each of the three angles of one is equal to a corresponding angle of the other. Similar triangles are applicable because corresponding sides of similar triangles are proportional. An example illustrating this idea is depicted in Figure 11-5.

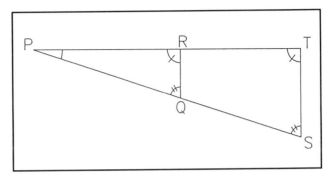

FIGURE 11-5. *The principle of similar triangles.*

In Figure 11-5, the side QR is parallel to the side ST. Thus we have the following relationships of angles:

Angle Q = Angle S
Angle R = Angle T

Since angle P obviously equals itself, we have two similar triangles in PQR and PST. We now know that the corresponding sides are proportional. Mathematically, we can write:

$$(PQ/PS) = (PR/PT) = (QR/ST)$$

The applications of similar triangles to the mathematical hobbyist will be illustrated by an example.

Suppose you are on the top of a mountain (to keep it simple, we'll use the same mountain as in the previous example). The mountain has an elevation of 3,900 feet above the surrounding tableland. In the distance, you sight another mountain. You sight the base of the mountain and obtain a value of 82° for the angle Θ in Figure 11-6.

Next, you take a ruler and hold it in front of you at a distance of one foot. You line the ruler up with the distant mountain and sight with one eye and a steady hand. You observe that the apparent distance from the mountain's base to its peak is 2 inches as seen on your ruler. Your ruler must be held vertically, since it is the vertical height you wish to estimate. This is to insure mathematically that line segments QR and ST are parallel.

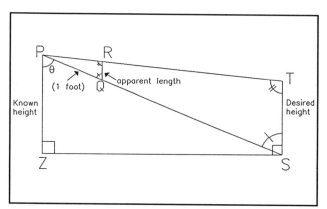

FIGURE 11-6. *Applying similar triangles to estimate the height of a distant mountain.*

To estimate the height of the mountain, two steps are necessary:

1. Determine the distance PS, i.e., the distance to the base of the mountain along your line of sight.
2. Make use of the similar triangles (PQR and PST) to compute the height of ST.

Let's get started with step 1. This problem is slightly different than the previous examples, since we are not worried about the distance along the ground (ZS), but the distance along your line of sight (PS). We can write:

$$PS = PZ/\cos(\theta), \text{ or } PS = 3{,}900/\cos(82°)$$

We estimate $\cos(82°)$ as being eight-tenths of the way between 0 and .174, or about .139. Then, we compute our distance PS as 3,900/.139 as a normal division problem to obtain approximately 28,060 feet.

In step 2, we make use of the similar triangles of Figure 11-6. We can write the following relationship:

$$(PS/PQ) = (QR/ST),$$
or (1 foot)/(28,060 feet) = (2 inches)/(height of mountain)

We see quickly that the height of the mountain is just one-sixth of 28,060 feet, or about 4,677 feet. This is the elevation above the tableland, which itself is at an elevation of 2,500 feet (in a previous example). We would therefore estimate the height above sea level of the mountain at 4,677 + 2,500 = 7,177 feet.

With this example, we will conclude this chapter. The purpose has been to show that you can have a good deal of enjoyment with these trigonometric functions.

The examples that I have used in this chapter have all come from the "wilderness" experiences. This is not to say that these are the only types of applications for the theory of this chapter. But the natural world seems to provide as good a backdrop as any for the use of trigonometric functions. I hope you can derive as much enjoyment from these problems as I do.

Chapter 12

Jack Kemp
and Evel Knievel

If you are familiar with the above names you're probably wondering what a mild-mannered former congressman from the state of New York (and recently appointed Director of the Office of Housing and Urban Development) has in common with a motorcycle daredevil. On top of that, you're probably also wondering what either of these guys has to do with trigonometry or math at all.

FOOTBALL PASSES

All right, I can understand your bewilderment. Let me start by talking about Jack Kemp. Those of you readers who live near Buffalo, New York or who are avid football fans may know that Jack Kemp was an outstanding quarterback of the Buffalo Bills during the mid-sixties. As a teenager living near Buffalo at the time, I loved football, and loved playing quarterback. I studied the style of Jack Kemp during every one of his games that I watched.

He was an amazing quarterback, not only because of his ability, but because of the unusual nature of his statistics. He guided his team to three championships in a row, was selected as the AFL's leading passer at least twice, and yet completed only about 43% of his passes.

His secret was the bomb. He would throw dozens of long bombs in each game. Even through only a small percentage of them would be completed, they all went for big gains. Jack Kemp knew how to throw the long ball.

I once watched him throw a ball 50 yards in the air. The play ended in a touchdown but was called back because of a holding penalty. On the replay, I held my protractor against the television screen and saw that he had thrown the ball at an arc (angle to the horizontal) of about 38°. How fast was the ball going? That was my next question. Unfortunately, at that time, I had not learned enough trigonometry to allow me to answer my question.

This problem is part of an interesting class called "projectile problems." Projectile problems are those problems that involve an object in "free fall," that is, under the sole influence of gravity. There are an incredible number of applications of projectile problems, one of which is the problem of throwing a football.

For purposes of this book, we will consider a projectile as a single moving point subject to the force of gravity. This relatively simple problem can be complicated enormously if the projectile is treated as a "rigid body," wobbling about in the air. The "rigid body" formulation, which is more precise, may be necessary for spacecraft or satellites. But for a simple football, thrown with a reasonably good spiral, we'll treat things simply as far as the world of physics goes.

Besides the force of gravity that acts on the football, there are really two other forces to consider. The first force is the force of the human being who rockets the football into the air. This force ceases its activity as soon as the ball leaves the passer's hand. We can think of the total result of this force as producing some initial velocity v and some initial angle of elevation Θ (representing the arc given to the ball).

The other force involved is air resistance. The force of air resistance always acts in a direction directly opposite to that of the motion of the body. Air resistance is an enormously complex force. Fortunately, for the vast majority of projectile problems, air resistance represents a negligibly small force and can be ignored. This will be the case with our football problem.

Ignoring air resistance, we can depict the football problem in the diagram Figure 12-1.

In Figure 12-1, the initial velocity v can be broken up into a vertical component ($v\sin(\Theta)$) and a horizontal component ($v\cos(\Theta)$). The force of gravity acts on the football continuously during its flight. This causes the football to move in a parabolic path as shown, since it is subjected to a constant acceleration downward.

Computing the Speed of the Ball

With this background, we can now start talking about equations of motion of the football. If we use units of feet for distance, then the acceleration of the football due to gravity is 32 feet per second

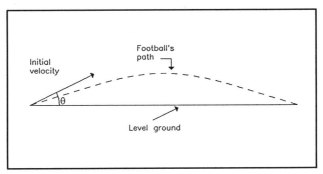

FIGURE 12-1. *The physics of throwing a football.*

every second. An object falling straight down would attain a speed of 32 feet per second after 1 second, 64 feet per second after 2 seconds, and so forth. A thrown football has associated with it these similar speeds as the contribution of gravity. But it also has the vertical speed given to it by the passer, which works against the speed due to gravity. At the highest point of the ball's flight, its vertical speed is 0 as both speeds cancel out in the vertical direction. From then on, the ever-accelerating vertical speed due to gravity becomes larger than the constant vertical speed imparted by the passer, and the football falls.

Let's denote the position of the football by y, expressed as a vertical coordinate, i.e., a height. The vertical height of the football can be expressed mathematically in Equation 12-1.

$$y = -16t^2 + vt\sin(\Theta) + y_0 \qquad \text{(Equation 12-1)}$$

Here, the parameter t is the time in seconds from the football's release. The term $vt\sin(\Theta)$ is the contribution of the passer to the vertical height of the football. The term $-16t^2$ is the contribution of gravity to the height of the football. It is negative since the acceleration of gravity is directed downwards. The y_0 term is a constant that indicates the initial height of the object. In the case of a thrown football, which is later caught at approximately the same height at which it is initially thrown, we will treat this term as 0.

But Equation 12-1 is only half of the story. It only describes the football's position vertically as a function of time. To get a complete description of the football's position as a function of time, we must also consider the horizontal position. The position of the football in the horizontal distance is given by Equation 12-2.

$$x = vt\cos(\Theta) + x_0 \qquad \text{(Equation 12-2)}$$

Here, x is the horizontal coordinate, in units of feet to be consistent. The constant x_0 allows for formulating a problem with the initial horizontal location being not equal to 0. This is unusual, however, as it is only seldom that one would wish to choose a value for x_0 other than 0.

Equations 12-1 and 12-2 can be used together to solve any projectile problem, assuming that the force of air resistance can be ignored. Now it is time to apply these equations to the solution of our football problem.

Recall that Jack Kemp's pass traveled 50 yards in the air and was caught at approximately the same height at which it was thrown. The initial angle Θ to the horizontal it was thrown at is 38°. It is the quantity v — the initial velocity of the ball — that we wish to compute.

Let us start by using Equation 12-1 to compute algebraically the length of time that the ball will be in the air as a function of v and Θ. Set $y_0 = 0$, which gives:

$y = -16t^2 + vt\sin(\Theta)$
or $16t^2 = vt\sin(\Theta)$ (at the point where $y = 0$ — the end of the flight)
$16t = v\sin(\Theta)$ (dividing by t ignoring the case when $t = 0$)
$t = [v\sin(\Theta)]/16$ (Equation 12-3)

Now, Equation 12-3 can be "plugged into" Equation 12-2. So, where the variable t appears in Equation 12-2 we will replace it with the expression of Equation 12-3. This gives us:

$x = [v^2\sin(\Theta) \cos (\Theta)] / 16$, assuming $x_0 = 0$ (Equation 12-4)

Solving the above for v gives:

$v = \sqrt{[16x/\sin(\Theta)\cos(\Theta)]}$ (Equation 12-5)

We can apply Equation 12-5 directly to solve the football problem since we know that $x = 50$ yards, or 150 feet, and Θ is 38°.

Let's start by computing the denominator of Equation 12-5. First, we can estimate $\cos(38°)$ as seven-fifteenths of the way between .707 ($\cos(45°)$) and .866 ($\cos(30°)$). This works out to approximately .781. $\sin(38°)$ will be about eight-fifteenths of the way from .500 to .707, or about .610.

For the product $\cos(\Theta)\sin(\Theta)$, we need to multiply .781 × .610. We get .476.

The numerator, 16x, is easily computed with $x = 150$ feet. This product is 2,400, and the entire fraction now has the value of 2,400/ .476, or about 5,042.

Finally, there is the matter of taking the square root of this. We note that $70^2 = 4,900$, and therefore that $71^2 = 4,900 + 70 + 71 = 5,041$. So, we'll call our estimate of v an even 71. To be consistent in our units, this is 71 feet per second.

A more meaningful set of units to most people would be miles per hour. To convert feet-per-second into miles-per-hour, multiply by 3,600 (seconds/hour) and divide by 5,280 (feet/mile). This multiplier (3,600/5,280) can be expressed as a lowest-terms fraction by 15/22, or decimally as .68.

We can use the decimal .68 number and multiply 71 x .68 to get the speed of Mr. Kemp's pass in miles per hour. We can multiply 71 x 68 as $(71 \times 69) - 71 = 4,899 - 71 = 4,828$. Placement of the decimal point gives us an answer of 48.3 miles per hour.

Obtaining this answer may have seemed like a good deal of work. In fact, in the process of solving this problem, we have laid the groundwork for the entire range of projectile problems. Equations 12-1 and 12-2 form the basis of all such problems. Equations 12-3, 12-4, and 12-5 are natural outgrowths of these two and can also be used to solve a wide range of problems.

Strictly speaking, we underestimated slightly the speed of Mr. Kemp's pass when we computed 48.3 miles per hour. The real speed would have been greater because a certain amount of air resistance would have had to be overcome. The real speed would also have depended on the local wind speed and wind direction.

MOTORCYCLE JUMPING

The second problem that we shall consider in this chapter is inspired by a former motorcycle daredevil named Evel Knievel. One of Mr. Knievel's stunts was to jump over a section of the Snake River Canyon in Idaho after he and his motorcycle were shot from a cannon-like device. The problem was a projectile problem-solver's dream. In fact, all such motorcycle stunts are interesting studies of projectile problems. Jumping over a string of barrels is an example of such a problem.

The barrel-jumping problem is solved directly from Equation 12-5. Here, x is the needed distance to clear the barrels and Θ is the angle of the ramp. We can solve for v — the speed the motorcyclist must attain to make his jump.

But the most spectacular stunt by far was jumping over the Snake River Canyon. Unfortunately, I do not know the exact distances involved in jumping this canyon. Rather than give false information about Mr. Knievel's feat, let's instead construct for our own purposes a new fictional problem along these lines.

A certain man on a motorcycle is about to be shot from a cannon over an abyss 1,000 feet across. The two sides of the abyss are of equal height. The cannon is capable of propelling the man and his motorcycle at a speed of 120 miles per hour. Assume that the winds are calm.

These are the facts of the problem. Two issues confront us here:

1. At what angle Θ should the cannon be aimed to maximize the distance that the man is hurled?
2. If he is shot at this angle Θ, will he make it?

We need to compute the answer to the first question in order to approach the second question with the known value of Θ.

If any readers have taken calculus, they will recognize the first question as a so-called maxima-minima problem. The basic principle behind this kind of problem is that the maxima and minima of any function are obtained at the points where its derivative is equal to 0. If you recall that the derivative of a function is just its slope at a certain point (i.e., its rate of change), then the points where this slope is 0 indicate where the function has either a "peak" or a "valley" (see Figure 12-2).

We can apply this principle to the function expressed in Equation 12-4. Here, in terms of our problem, v is a given constant (120 miles per hour), and we have therefore a situation of x being a function of Θ. We can rewrite Equation 12-4 to illuminate this point:

$x = K\sin(\Theta)\cos(\Theta)$, where $K = v^2/16$.

Maximizing the quantity $K\sin(\Theta)\cos(\Theta)$ therefore amounts to finding the value of Θ for which the product $\sin(\Theta)\cos(\Theta)$ is maximized. This, in turn, means setting the derivative of the quantity $\sin(\Theta)\cos(\Theta)$ equal to 0.

The derivative of $\sin(\Theta)\cos(\Theta)$ is $\cos^2(\Theta) - \sin^2(\Theta)$. This derivative is 0 whenever $\cos(\Theta) = \sin(\Theta)$ or when $\cos(\Theta) = -\sin(\Theta)$. Since the problem statement implies that Θ be in the range of 0° to 90°,

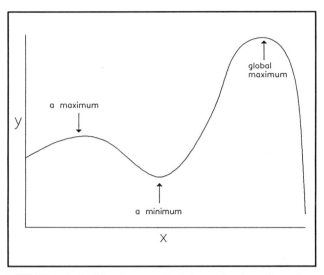

FIGURE 12-2. *Maxima and minima of a function of x.*

we can rule out the second case. Therefore, we know the only angle for which cos(Θ) = sin(Θ) is 45°.

How do we know whether this is a minimum or a maximum? In this case we know by intuition that it is a maximum. Certainly, a greater distance could be obtained by firing at 45°, instead of, say, at 0°.

In a problem where it is not so obvious if a point is a minimum or a maximum, the rule of calculus states that you should look at the second derivative of the point in question. If the second derivative is positive (i.e., the first derivative is increasing), then the point is a minimum. Similarly, if the second derivative is negative, the point is a maximum. In the unusual case in which the second derivative is 0, the point is neither a maximum nor a minimum, but a kind of "bump" or glitch (see Figure 12-3). The mathematical term for such an occurrence is "saddle point."

Well, back to the motorcyclist being shot from the cannon. We've determined that he should be shot at an angle of 45°. The next issue is whether or not he will make it.

The distance that he will cover is figured directly from Equation 12-4. Here we know Θ to be 45°, and the product sin(Θ)cos(Θ) to be $(.707)^2 = .5$. We know v is 120 miles per hour. We need to convert this to feet-per-second to be used in Equation 12-4, so we divide 120/.68. This gives 176 feet/second (perhaps more easily converted

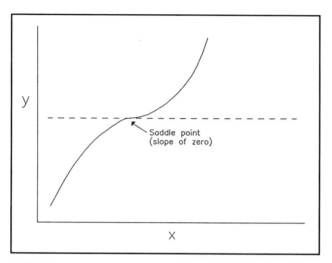

FIGURE 12-3. *A first derivative of zero which is neither a maximum nor a minimum.*

by using the fractional ratio 15/22, instead of .68). We can now plug the numbers into Equation 12-4 to obtain the following:

$$x = (176)^2 (.5) / 16$$

Before thrusting ourselves into this problem headlong, we can simplify it somewhat. We note that $(176)^2 / 16$ is just $(44)^2$. Of course, $(44)^2$ is just $2,025 - 45 - 44 = 1,936$. We multiply $1,936 \times .5$ to obtain 968 feet, a bit less than the canyon's width of 1,000 feet. Our unnamed daredevil will come heartbreakingly close.

PROJECTILE PROBLEMS

In the course of solving this problem, we discovered an interesting fact about projectiles. This is that a projectile's horizontal distance is maximized when it is initially shot at an angle of 45°. This is true for all projectiles that reach the ground at the same height from which they are propelled (this premise is the basis for Equation 12-4).

Interestingly, there are exceptions to this rule. One interesting exception comes from striking a baseball with a bat. We can ask the following question: If a baseball bat of circular cross-section is swung along a horizontal, level plane, at what angle Θ should the ball be initially propelled to maximize its horizontal flight distance?

Here, the direction of the force is parallel to the ground. Therefore, the ball is propelled at an angle Θ to the direction of the applied force (denote the magnitude of the force by F). The physics of impact collisions tells us that the actual force instrumental in imparting velocity to the ball will be $F\cos(\Theta)$. The initial velocity v of the ball will then be a function of Θ and not regarded as a constant. In particular, we would have $v = FK\cos(\Theta)$, where K is a constant to be determined by the physics of the problem.

Plugging this value of v into Equation 12-4 gives us:

$$x = (FK)^2\cos^2(\Theta)\sin(\Theta)\cos(\Theta) / 16$$
or $x = K_1\cos^3(\Theta)\sin(\Theta)$, where $K_1 = (FK)^2/16$.

Since the quantity expressed as K_1 can be treated as a constant, our baseball batter's problem is one of finding the value of Θ for which $\cos^3(\Theta)\sin(\Theta)$ is maximized.

We can derive the derivative of $\cos^3(\Theta)\sin(\Theta)$ as $\cos^4(\Theta) - 3\cos^2(\Theta)\sin^2(\Theta)$. (See Appendix A.)

Computing the values of Θ that set this derivative to 0 appears not at all easy. Yet the task is simplified if we first factor out $\cos^2(\Theta)$. This gives us:

$$\cos^2(\Theta)[\cos^2(\Theta) - 3\sin^2(\Theta)] = 0$$

The above is equal to 0 in two instances:

1. When $\cos^2(\Theta) = 0$, i.e., when $\Theta = 90°$, but this is clearly a minimum.
2. When $\cos^2(\Theta) - 3\sin^2(\Theta) = 0$.

The quantity in the second case can be analyzed by making the simplifying substitution:

$$z = \sin(\Theta),$$

which implies that $\sin^2(\Theta) = z^2$ and that $\cos^2(\Theta) = 1 - z^2$. We can now solve the simpler problem for z:

$$(1 - z^2) - 3z^2 = 0,$$

which gives us $4z^2 = 1$, or $z = \frac{1}{2}$.

The value of Θ is obtained by making the reverse substitution:

$$\Theta = \arcsin(z), \text{ or } \Theta = \arcsin(.5)$$

from which Θ is determined as $30°$. This is the angle at which the ball should leave the bat in order to travel the maximum distance.

There are countless more examples of projectile problems — many that are noticeable in day-to-day living. It is one of the more interesting areas of physics and trigonometry.

Chapter 13

Our Curved Earth

To me, some of the most fascinating problems of all come from air travel. To many people, air travel is a boring activity. To me, it is exciting. I am always at a window seat, looking out at the ground, trying to guess where I am or what small town is off to the side.

Many interesting and surprisingly simple calculations can be done in an airplane with the aid of only a protractor and ruler, as in the problems of Chapter 11. Distances to objects along the Earth's surface can be approximated using the methods of Chapter 11, assuming that you know the height at which your plane is flying. Distances along the Earth can also be computed by using a pocket ruler and the method of similar triangles explained in Chapter 11. Since we have already discussed these problems in an earlier chapter, we won't do them again here. But we will talk some about the unique kind of problems that air travel offers.

ESTIMATING HORIZON DISTANCES

One such problem is estimating how far you can see to the horizon. The distance to the horizon depends entirely on the altitude of the viewer. Figure 13-1 illustrates this.

In Figure 13-1, the distance we wish to compute is indicated by d and is measured along the curved surface of the Earth. If the angle Θ of Figure 13-1 is measured in radians, then the distance d will be $R\Theta$, where R is the radius of the Earth, which we assume to be a perfect sphere.

In Figure 13-1, our present location is indicated by the point P. The point C is the center of the Earth, and T is the point where our line of sight is tangent to the Earth's surface. The point T represents the farthest point that we can see on the Earth's surface. It is the horizon.

Note from geometry that the triangle CPT is a right triangle,

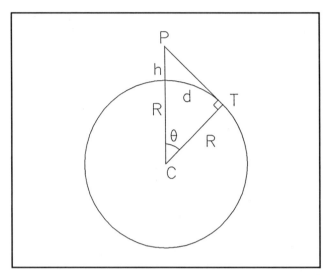

FIGURE 13-1. *Computing the distance to the horizon.*

since all radii are perpendicular to tangent lines where they intersect on the perimeter. The hypotenuse of this triangle is R + h, where h is your present altitude. We note that:

$\cos(\Theta) = R/(R + h)$

In theory, we could actually perform the division $R/(R + h)$ and go about taking the arccos of this quantity to find Θ. In practice, this is not easy, since the quantity $R/(R + h)$ is so close to 1.

The best thing to do here is to expand the function $\cos(\Theta)$ into a Taylor Series when Θ is very close to 0. If we express Θ in units of radians, then the derivative of $\cos(\Theta)$ is $-\sin(\Theta)$, and the second derivative of $\cos(\Theta)$ is $-\cos(\Theta)$. We can write a Taylor Series formulation as follows, when Θ is expressed in radians:

$\cos(x + \Theta) = \cos(x) - \sin(x)\Theta - \cos(x)\Theta^2/2 + $ (smaller terms)

If x in the above equation is 0, then $\cos(x)$ is 1 and $\sin(x)$ is 0. We can use these values to derive the Taylor Series for angles that are close to 0.

$\cos(\Theta) = (1 - \Theta^2)/2$, as we set x to 0.

We can plug $(1 - \Theta^2)/2$ in for $\cos(\Theta)$ in the previous relation to obtain the following:

$(1 - \Theta^2)/2 = R/(R + h)$
or $\Theta^2/2 = 1 - (R/R + h))$
$\Theta^2 = 2h/(R + h)$
$\Theta = \sqrt{[2h/R]}$, approximating $h/(R + h)$ as h/R

The final approximation is accurate, since h is extremely small compared to R; that is, the altitude is very small compared to the radius of the Earth.

Now it's time to talk about units and numbers. The radius of the Earth at the equator is about 3,960 miles. The polar radius is a few miles less, but we'll use R as equal to 3,960 miles.

Our horizon distance $R\Theta$ now becomes:

$$R\Theta = R \sqrt{[2h/R]} = 3,960 \sqrt{[h/1,980]}$$

If our altitude h is expressed in feet (and it almost always is), we need to convert it to miles in order to divide it by the radius R, which is in miles. This involves a division by 5,280 and gives us:

$$R\Theta = 3,960 \sqrt{[h/(5,280 \times 1,980)]}$$

A final formula can be obtained by grouping together all the constants. We want to divide 3,960 by the square root of 5,280 × 1,980 to accomplish this. Everything then reduces to:

horizon distance = $1.2 \sqrt{h}$ (Equation 13-1)

This incredibly simple formula can be used to estimate any horizon distance in miles, given the viewer's altitude in feet.

Some Practice

Let's take a few examples. I'm 5'10" tall. My eye level is about 4" lower, or at about 5'6" above the ground. If I am standing in a flat area with no obstacles to my sight, how far can I see? Here, my value of h (in feet) is 5.5 (remember, 6" is .5 of a foot). The square root of 5.5 can be approximated as 2.345 (using $2.3^2 = 5.29$ and $2.4^2 = 5.76$).

Multiplying this by 1.2 gives about 2.8 miles as my horizon distance.

If you are atop a mountain 6,000 feet in height, the same formula applies with h = 6,000. We can estimate the square root of 6,000 by noting that 77^2 is 5,929 ($75^2 + 4 \times 76$), and that 78^2 is 155 more than 5,929. So, the square root of 6,000 is linearly approximated as 77 plus 71/155, or about 77.46.

The horizon distance is then 77.46 × 1.2 miles, or about 92.9 miles.

A short aside — how do you quickly multiply any number by 1.2? I would suggest multiplying the number by .2 (by doubling it and then dividing by 10) and then adding this number to itself. Thus, in the last example, we might multiply 77.46 by .2 by doubling 77.46 to get 154.92, dividing by 10 to get 15.49, and finally adding 77.46 + 15.49.

As a last example, how far can you see out of the window of an airplane flying at 37,000 feet? In this case, we must first compute the square root of 37,000. This is not quite that easy. We can start with $190^2 = 36,100$. 192^2 is therefore this plus 4(191) = 36,100 + 764 = 36,864. The difference between this and 37,000 is then 136. The difference between this and the square of 193 is 192 + 193 = 385. So, we can linearly approximate this square root as about 192 + (136/385). We should perform this division quickly without doing a lot of arduous work trying to get extra decimal places that will be dropped later anyway. We can roughly guess the fraction to be slightly more than a third, so that our square root approximation is about 192.35.

We can multiply this by 1.2 in the manner just described. Thus, we can start by doubling 192.35 to get 384.7, and then divide by 10 for 38.47. The sum 192.35 + 38.47 gives an answer of 230.82 miles.

This is a remarkable result if you pause to reflect on it. On a clear day, if you look out the right side of an airplane, and then out the left side, the two farthest points that you see could be 460 miles apart. Conceivably, you could see Denver, Colorado and Omaha, Nebraska out of opposite windows of the same airplane at the same time.

It is even more remarkable to imagine what things would be like if the entire airplane were covered with windows (quite impossible for structural reasons). The view might seem frightening to air-traveling neophytes. The view that you would have would be an approximate circle on the Earth's surface with a radius of 230 miles. The area of this circle would be about 3.1416×230^2, or about 160,000 square miles. This is very close to the area of the state of California.

Sometimes I enjoy bringing a detailed map or set of maps with me on an air trip. As the pilot announces our location, I find it on the map, and estimate where certain other landmarks should be.

Sometimes the methods of Chapter 11 can be used to spot even relatively small landmarks with the aid of a protractor.

ESTIMATING DISTANCES

Another interesting problem of air travel is estimating the Great Circle distances between cities. The process of solving this problem gives us a good introduction to spherical trigonometry.
The general method is simply illustrated in Figure 13-2.

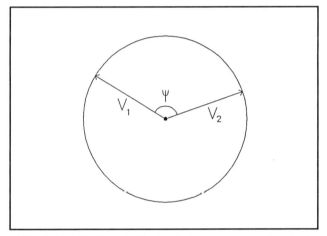

FIGURE 13-2. *Great Circle distances are estimated from the angle between two vectors.*

In Figure 13-2, two vectors v_1 and v_2 are drawn to two cities from the center of the Earth. Denote by Ψ (Greek letter "psi") the angle between these two vectors. Then $R\Psi$, where R is the radius of the Earth and Ψ is measured in radians, is the desired Great Circle distance between the two cities.

Our general method will be to determine this angle Ψ in radians, which, when multiplied by R, will give us the desired distance.

We may assume that we know the latitudes and longitudes of the two cities. These numbers, along with the radius of the Earth R are the spherical coordinates. Let's define the following notations to work with:

Θ_1 = the latitude of city 1
Φ_1 = the longitude of city 1
Θ_2 = the latitude of city 2
Φ_2 = the longitude of city 2

We shall adopt the following conventions:

1. North latitude is indicated by a positive angle; south by a negative angle.
2. East longitude is considered positive; west is negative.

We will also require a rectangular coordinate system with coordinates x, y, and z. The origin of this coordinate system is the center of the Earth. Define the coordinates x, y, and z as follows:

x = the coordinate measured along the line from the center of the Earth to the point on the equator that corresponds to 0° longitude.

y = the coordinate measured along the line from the center of the Earth to the point on the equator that corresponds to +90° longitude.

z = the coordinate measured along the line from the center of the Earth to the North Pole.

With a little geometric sweat, we can write equations for x, y, and z in terms of their spherical counterparts. This gives us the following three relationships:

$$x_1 = R\cos(\Theta_1)\cos(\Phi_1)$$
$$y_1 = R\cos(\Theta_1)\sin(\Phi_1)$$
$$z_1 = R\sin(\Theta_1)$$

Here we have used x_1, y_1, and z_1 as the rectangular coordinates of city 1. An exactly analogous set of relationships can be written for city 2, where x_2, y_2, and z_2 are expressed in terms of Θ_2 and Φ_2.

Now the vectors v_1 and v_2 can be written in terms of the rectangular coordinates just defined. For notation, and to stay theoretically sound, we need to define i, j, and k as vectors of unit length in the directions of x, y, and z coordinates respectively. Then we can write:

$$v_1 = x_1 i + y_1 j + z_1 k$$
$$v_2 = x_2 i + y_2 j + z_2 k$$

Given this formulation, the vector dot product, written $v_1 \cdot v_2$, is a scalar quantity equal to $x_1 x_2 + y_1 y_2 + z_1 z_2$.

But a neat theorem from vector calculus tells us that the dot product $v_1 \cdot v_2$ can also be computed by an alternate method. The alternate computation is to multiply the length of v_1 times the length of v_2 times the cosine of the angle between the two vectors. Conveniently for us, the lengths of v_1 and v_2 are both equal to the radius of the Earth R. The angle between v_1 and v_2 is just the angle Ψ, which we want to determine.

The whole key to this problem is equating the two calculations for the dot product. This gives us the following algebraic relationship:

$$x_1 x_2 + y_1 y_2 + z_1 z_2 = R^2 \cos(\Psi)$$

The next step is to substitute Θ's and Φ's for x's, y's, and z's. This can be done using the set of relationships between rectangular and spherical coordinates. The resulting expression is a bit lengthy:

$$R\cos(\Theta_1)\cos(\Phi_1)R\cos(\Theta_2)\cos(\Phi_2) +$$
$$R\cos(\Theta_1)\sin(\Phi_1)R\cos(\Theta_2)\sin(\Phi_2)$$
$$+ R\sin(\Theta_1)R\sin(\Theta_2) = R^2\cos(\Psi)$$

The first thing we can do is factor out R^2. This simplifies things a bit:

$$\cos(\Theta_1)\cos(\Theta_2)[\cos(\Phi_1)\cos(\Phi_2) +$$
$$\sin(\Phi_1)\sin(\Phi_2)] + \sin(\Theta_1)\sin(\Theta_2) = \cos(\Psi)$$

Here, we can make use of the trigonometric identity for expressing the cosine of the difference of two angles. The identity has the following form:

$$\cos(\Phi_1 - \Phi_2) = \cos(\Phi_1)\cos(\Phi_2) + \sin(\Phi_1)\sin(\Phi_2)$$

Use of this identity can simplify things even more:

$$\cos(\Theta_1)\cos(\Theta_2)\cos(\Phi_1 - \Phi_2) + \sin(\Theta_1)\sin(\Theta_2) = \cos(\Psi)$$
$$\text{(Equation 13-2)}$$

Equation 13-2 gives us the method for finding the Great Circle distance between any two cities on the Earth. The method can be summarized as follows:

1. Record the latitude and longitude of the two cities. Denote these numbers by the Θ and Φ symbols of Equation 13-2.
2. Apply Equation 13-2, computing the left side, with all the Θ and Φ values known.
3. Take the arccos of the quantity computed in step 2.
4. Convert the angle computed in step 3 to radians by multiplying degrees by .0175.

5. Multiply the angle in radians by 3,960 miles, the approximate radius of the Earth.

Some Practice

Let's illustrate by computing the air mile Great Circle distance from New York to London. We'll use the step-by-step approach outlined above.

Step 1. Record the latitudes and longitudes of the two cities. Arbitrarily selecting New York as city 1 and London as city 2, we obtain the following:

$$\Theta_1 = 41° \qquad \Phi_1 = -74°$$
$$\Theta_2 = 52° \qquad \Phi_2 = 0°$$

Step 2. We employ the lengthy process of computing the left side of Equation 13-2, namely the quantity $\cos(\Theta_1)\cos(\Theta_2)\cos(\Phi_1 - \Phi_2) + \sin(\Theta_1)\sin(\Theta_2)$. Using the methods of linear interpolation, we obtain estimates as follows:

$$\cos(\Theta_1) = \cos(41°) = .771$$
$$\cos(\Theta_2) = \cos(52°) = .609$$
$$\cos(\Phi_1 - \Phi_2) = \cos(-74°) = .275$$
$$\sin(\Theta_1) = \sin(41°) = .651$$
$$\sin(\Theta_2) = \sin(52°) = .818$$

The multiplications involved in computing the left side of Equation 13-2 are lengthy, but computable by the standard multiplication methods elaborated in previous chapters. We will spare the reader the details of these calculations.

After performing the necessary arithmetic, we obtain approximately .652, which is our estimate for $\cos(\Psi)$.

Step 3. We compute arccos(.652). We note that $\cos(60°) = .500$ and $\cos(45°) = .707$. We therefore estimate arccos(.652) as approximately $152/207$ of the way from $60°$ to $45°$. This works out to about $50°$.

Step 4. We compute this value in radians by multiplying $50°$ times .0175 radians per degree. This is a relatively easy calculation. The result is .875 radians.

Step 5. We multiply the angle in radians by the radius of the Earth. Thus, our distance in miles is approximately 3,960 × .875.

This works out to 3,465 miles. Amazingly, *The World Almanac* reports this distance as 3,469 miles.

Of course, this method — although more laborious than looking up a number in an almanac — provides more flexibility. Many cities or points on the Earth are not listed in almanacs or tables. But your calculations have no such limitations imposed on them. You can determine the distance between any location, large city or small town.

A Simpler Method

Is this method too laborious for you? If so, a simpler, more approximate method is possible, but you will need a globe, a piece of string, and a ruler. The method is as follows:

Step 1. Determine the scale of your globe. The globe's scale means how many miles on the Earth correspond to one inch on your globe. Determining this number is easiest if you know your globe's diameter. You can then divide the Earth's diameter (7,920 miles) by the globe's diameter (usually 12″ or 16″) to get the scale of the globe. If you don't know your globe's diameter, you can calculate it by measuring the globe's circumference and dividing by π.

Step 2. Determine the Great Circle route between the two cities. Stretch the string taut between the two points. The path that the taut string takes is the Great Circle route, and the length of string necessary to connect the points is the Great Circle distance on your globe's scale.

Step 3. Calculate the Great Circle distance on the Earth's scale by measuring the length of string needed and multiplying by the scale of your globe.

This method is subject to two types of error — inaccuracies on the globe and human inaccuracies in measuring the length of string necessary to connect the points. But if you have the necessary equipment, this method offers simplicity and accuracy to a good first approximation.

ESTIMATING SUNRISE AND SUNSET TIMES

A globe, a ruler, and string are the tools that can allow you to solve a vast array of problems, perhaps more than you realize. One class of such problems involves the position of the sun. Believe it or not, you can calculate the time of sunrise or sunset on any day of the year at any point on Earth using a globe, a piece of string, a ruler, and a graphic device called an analemma.

The analemma (Figure 13-3) plots the location of the sun for each day of the year. The position of the sun is specified in terms of its latitude and longitude. Given the sun's latitude and longitude at some particular time, we know that the sun is directly overhead the point on the Earth's surface with the same latitude and longitude.

The vertical axis of the analemma is used to determine the sun's latitude. The horizontal axis is used to determine the sun's longitude.

To determine the sun's latitude, simply find the date on the analemma's curve and read off the corresponding value in degrees along the vertical axis.

Determining the sun's longitude is a bit more work. On any day, the sun is approximately at 0° longitude at twelve noon Greenwich Mean Time. The sun moves westward at 15° per hour. So the sun is approximately at 15° west longitude at 1 p.m. GMT; at 30° west longitude at 2 p.m. GMT; and so forth. If you don't like GMT, you can remember that at twelve noon local standard time (or 1 p.m. local daylight savings time) the sun's longitude is approximately the appropriate multiple of 15° corresponding to your time zone. (Example: the appropriate longitude in the Eastern U.S.A. time zone is 75°.)

The horizontal axis of the analemma tells you by how much the sun is ahead or behind the clock on any particular day. For example, we can see from the analemma that on August 20th, the sun is approximately 4 minutes ahead of the clock. So, where ordinarily the sun would arrive at 0° longitude at twelve noon GMT, on August 20th it gets there instead at 11:56. The sun moves westward 15° per hour, or 1° in 4 minutes. This means that at twelve noon GMT (or 6 a.m. Eastern Daylight Savings Time), the sun will be at longitude 1° west. Its latitude will be 13° north, which can be read directly off the analemma's vertical axis.

Sunrise and sunset times may be determined by using the analemma and the fact that sunrise and sunset occur when the sun's position is 90° distant from the observer's position. Here 90° corresponds to the angle Ψ from Figure 13-2. It is the angle subtended at the Earth's center by the location of the observer and the location of the sun.

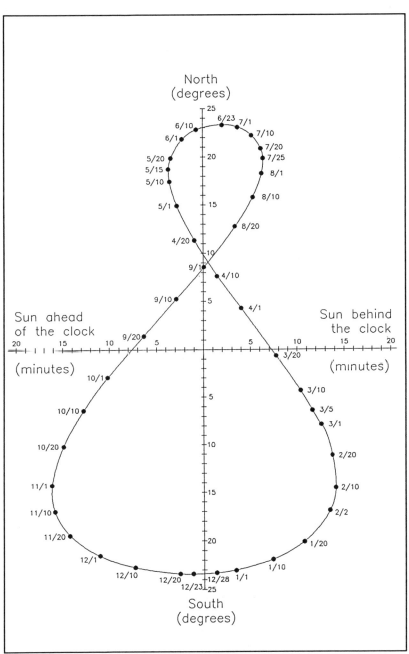

FIGURE 13-3. *Sun's position for each day of the year.*

A key idea helps us here. If we look at any Great Circle segment on the earth's surface, its length is proportional to the angle that is subtended by it at the earth's center. For example, the earth's equator is a Great Circle whose length is equal to the earth's circumference and whose corresponding subtended angle is 360°. Any Great Circle segment with a length ¼ of the earth's circumference will have a corresponding subtended angle of 360° / 4 = 90°, and so forth. Thus it is common to speak of the length of a Great Circle segment in terms of the degrees of its subtended angle. The length of a Great Circle segment in degrees can be computed by measuring its linear length, taking the fraction of this linear length to the circumference, and finally determining the approximate proportional part of 360°.

Some Practice

As an example, we'll find the time of sunrise in Cairo, Egypt on November 10th.

Step 1. Determine from the analemma that on November 10th the sun's latitude is 17° south and that it is 16 minutes ahead of the clock.

Step 2. Take a piece of string that is 90° long. 90° corresponds to one quarter of your globe's circumference.

Step 3. With one end of the string fixed at Cairo and the rest of the string stretching eastward, hold the string taut to determine where the other end (90° from Cairo) intersects the line of 17° south latitude. You should find this to be around longitude 110° east in the Indian Ocean northwest of Australia.

Step 4. Find the nearest "hour line" (increment of 15° of longitude). In this case, this is 105° east. The sun will be at longitude 105° east at 11:44 a.m. local standard time, since it is 16 minutes ahead of the clock. Since the sun moves westward at the rate of 1° per 4 minutes, it will be at longitude 110° east 20 minutes earlier, or at 11:24 local standard time. 11:24 local time for the hour line 105° east corresponds to 6:24 a.m. local time at Cairo's hour line (30° east). This is our answer.

The inquiring reader may wonder how to do this problem mathematically. The solution is to use Equation 13-2 in the following manner:

- Use for Θ_1 and Φ_1 the latitude and longitude of Cairo.
- Use for Θ_2 $-17°$ — the latitude of the sun on November 10th.
- Set the angle Ψ at 90° — the required angular displacement between the sun and Cairo at sunrise.
- Solve for the unknown Φ_2 — the sun's longitude. You will get two solutions. The eastward solution will correspond to the sunrise, and the westward solution will correspond to the sunset. Select the eastward solution, use the analemma to determine the sun is 14 minutes ahead of the clock, and apply step 4 to determine the sunrise time.

As a second example, we can determine the elevation of the sun above the horizon in Pittsburgh, Pennsylvania at 5 p.m on September 5th.

Step 1. Use the analemma to determine that on September 5th the sun's latitude is 7° north and it is 1 minute ahead of the clock.

Step 2. Note that on September 5th, Pittsburgh will be in daylight savings time. In standard time, this is 4 p.m. We will work out the problem using 4 p.m. standard time.

Step 3. The closest hour line to Pittsburgh is 75° west. The sun is 1 minute ahead of the clock, so it will reach this point at 11:59 a.m. standard time.

Step 4. At 3:59 p.m. Eastern Standard Time, the sun will have moved 60° westward and will then be at longitude 135° west. At 4:00 EST the sun will be at longitude 135.25° west and, of course, 7° north latitude.

Step 5. Stretch the string from Pittsburgh to the sun's location, as computed in step 4. You should find that the length of string necessary should be about 1/6 of the circumference of your globe, or about 60°. This means that the sun will be about 60° from being directly overhead, or, in other words, 30° above the horizon. The direction that the string takes in leaving Pittsburgh indicates the compass heading of the sun.

Again, we can do this problem mathematically using Equation 13-2. We can set Θ_1 and Φ_1 equal to the latitude and longitude of Pittsburgh, set Θ_2 and Φ_2 equal to the latitude and longitude of the sun (as determined from the analemma), and solve for Ψ, which gives us the angular displacement from the vertical. 90° - Ψ will be the angle of elevation over the horizon.

DETERMINING POSITION ON EARTH

An interesting problem is to determine your position on the Earth's surface by watching the sun. There are many different ways of doing this. I will present three different methods, each assuming a minimal amount of measuring equipment.

Method One

This method requires an analemma, a globe, a watch, and a string.

Step 1. Observe the sun for one day, noting the times of sunrise and sunset.

Step 2. Use the analemma to determine the sun's latitude and longitude for the sunrise and the sunset times.

Step 3. Your location will be 90° distant from the sun at sunrise and sunset times. Use a piece of string with a length of 90°, i.e., ¼ of your globe's circumference. Sweep out a circle of 90° centered at the sun's location at sunrise. This circle will be all the points on the Earth that are 90° from the sunrise point. Sweep out a second circle in the same way but centered about the sunset point. The two circles will intersect in two points. One of these points will be your location.

Step 4. Of the two points, one will lie to the north of the sun's latitude, and one will lie to the south. By observing the sun's path during the day, you can easily determine if the sun moves from east to west across the northern sky or the southern sky. Then you will know which one of the points is your location.

Method Two

This method requires a stick, a ruler, an analemma, and a watch.

Step 1. Insert the stick into the ground so that it stands up vertically.

Step 2. Monitor the length of the shadow cast by the stick on the ground. When the length of this shadow is shortest, then this instant of time is high noon at your location. As closely as possible, note on your watch the time of day high noon occurs. Also note the length of the shadow at high noon.

Step 3. From the analemma, determine the sun's latitude and longitude at the time of high noon.

Step 4. At high noon the longitude of the sun equals your longitude.

Step 5. Your latitude can be determined by the length of the shadow cast at high noon. See Figure 13-4.

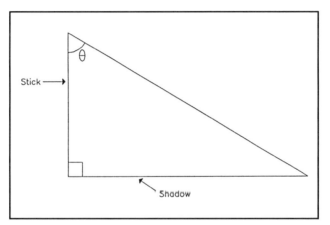

FIGURE 13-4. *Determining your latitude based on the length of the shadow cast at high noon.*

In Figure 13-4, the angle Θ is the difference between your latitude and the sun's latitude. You can solve for Θ as:

Θ = arctan(length of shadow/length of stick)

Θ can be determined by simply using the methods of Chapter 10.

Step 6. If the sun passes through the northern sky, then your latitude will be south of the sun. If the sun passes through the southern sky, your latitude will be north of the sun. This will let you determine the directional sense of Θ, the difference between your latitude and the sun's.

Method Three

This method requires a compass, an analemma, a watch, and a protractor or sextant.

Step 1. At any time of day, measure the elevation angle of the sun over the horizon and the compass heading to the sun.

Step 2. Use the analemma to determine the sun's latitude and longitude at the time of sighting.

Step 3. Use known formulas from spherical trigonometry to determine your position. Figure 13-5 illustrates the situation.

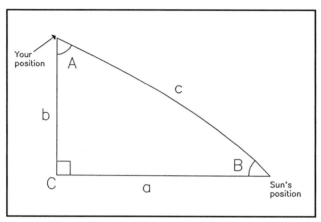

FIGURE 13-5. *Using a spherical triangle to depict your position in relation to the sun's position.*

A spherical triangle is much different from a triangle in the plane. Its angles normally don't add up to 180°. Its legs are not measured in units of length but in degrees of arc (subtended from the Earth's center). In Figure 13-5, we are able to determine angle A based on the compass heading of the sun. In Figure 13-5, this angle is arbitrarily drawn to measure displacement from the southerly direction. We also know leg c from our measurement of the sun's elevation above the horizon. Leg c will be 90° minus the angle of elevation. We also know that angle C is a right angle.

From the theory of right spherical triangles, we can now employ two relations. First, we can use the following relation to determine the leg a:

$\sin(a) = [\sin(A)][\sin(c)]$

Now, knowing the value of leg a, we can apply a second relation to find the value of leg b:

$\sin(b) = \tan(a)/\tan(A)$

Referring to Figure 13-5, leg a is the difference between your longitude and the sun's longitude. Leg b is the difference between your latitude and the sun's latitude.

The third method is perhaps the easiest operationally, but it does have an imperfection. Taking the compass heading of the sun is not an accurate procedure because a compass points to the magnetic north pole, not to the true north pole. If you know to an approximation where you are (for example in the North Atlantic Ocean, near the Azores), then you can use navigational charts to tell you your "magnetic deviation," i.e., the difference between the compass's north and the true north. If you have no idea where you are, you should probably use one of the other methods.

RISE IN SEA LEVEL

Significant problems involving our Earth can come from the news. One interesting problem is inspired by the current concerns about global warming. Supposing that all the ice in Greenland were to melt, how disastrous would the results be? Mathematically, the following question can be posed: If all the ice in Greenland melted, what would be the resulting increase in the height of ocean water?

The World Almanac lists the area of Greenland as 840,000 square miles. Not all of this is ice-capped. The same *World Almanac* gives the area of ice-capped Greenland as 705,234 square miles. It also gives the average thickness of the ice as 1,000 feet, or about .2 miles. Thus, the total volume of ice can be computed as about 140,000 cubic miles.

When ice melts, the volume of liquid water created is about 9/10 the volume of the ice. This is because the density of ice is approximately 9/10 the density of liquid water. Thus 9/10 of an iceberg lies underwater.

If 140,000 cubic miles of ice were to melt, it would produce approximately 126,000 cubic miles of liquid water. So, we have 126,000 cubic miles of water to spread out equally among all the oceans.

We now need to compute the area of the oceans. First, we can approximate the total surface area of the Earth by the formula $4\pi r^2$, if we assume that the Earth is a perfect sphere. For ease of calculation, let's take r to be 4,000 miles. The square of this is 16 million. Multiply this first by 4 to obtain 64 million, and then by π (about 3.14) to get approximately 200,000,000 square miles.

We can use the commonly applied rule that approximately three-fourths of this area is water. Then we have an estimate of 150,000,000 square miles as the total water area of the earth.

At this point, we have 126,000 cubic miles of additional water to be spread equally over 150,000,000 square miles of existing water. The gain in the height of the ocean in miles would be 126,000 divided by 150,000,000. This gives about .008 miles — or just about four feet.

Note

The data used for the construction of the analemma in this chapter came from *The World Almanac*. On some globes, particularly older ones, analemmas are often drawn and scaled.

Chapter 14

Problems in Probability

Anyone who has ever listened to a weather report or studied base-ball players' batting averages has had some exposure to probability. Statements like "There's a 40% chance of rain today" or "Joe Schmaltz is batting .385 with runners in scoring position" are rou-tinely broadcast to millions of people daily through the media.

But probability has a much greater role in our lives, even if we may only give it passing consideration. Have you ever taken a risk in crossing a busy street against the light? Have you ever disobeyed a doctor's order? Have you ever driven too fast to get someplace important? Then you were making a decision based on probability. You have, in effect, estimated the probability of a bad outcome to your risk-taking and decided it was worth the risk. You can gain insight into these risks by trying to associate a number to the risk. For example, when crossing a busy street against the light, you might estimate the fraction of people who do this every day and are seriously hurt or killed. Is it maybe one in 5,000? Is it worth it?

The point is that probability is everywhere. Wherever there is uncertainty, there is probability. In this chapter we will discuss many problems related to gambling, sports, and other recreational pursuits. We will do this because these fields provide a good vehicle for learning probability theory. But the reader is well-advised to appreciate the uses of probability in day-to-day living.

In this chapter, we will discuss problems in three different areas of probability theory: event counting, sequential events, and pro-babilistic decision-making.

EVENT COUNTING

Suppose you roll two dice. What is the probability that the total of the dice will be 9 or greater? This is an example of a problem that can be solved by event counting. This type of problem is characterized as having a number of different outcomes, all occurring with equal likelihood. A total of 7 occurs most frequently, and a total of 1 or 12 is least frequent. But individual values on each die do occur with equal likelihood. The thirty-six possible combinations of individual values on each die can be used as our set of equally probable outcomes.

Out of these thirty-six, a 9 can occur in four ways (6-3, 5-4, 4-5, 3-6), a 10 in three ways (6-4, 5-5, 4-6), an 11 in two ways (6-5, 5-6), and a 12 in one way (6-6). To determine the probability of a favorable outcome, we divide the number of favorable outcomes (4 + 3 + 2 + 1) by the total number of outcomes to obtain 10/36, or 5/18.

Another problem in this category is to estimate the probability that eight horses in a horse race finish in the exact order of their post positions, i.e., 1-2-3-4-5-6-7-8. For simplicity's sake, assume that all horses are of equal abilities. Here there is just one favorable outcome — the ordering 1-2-3-4-5-6-7-8. But in how many different ways can you order them? There are eight possible first-place finishers; after the first-place finisher is selected, there are seven possible second-place finishers, then six thirds, and so forth. The total number of ways is then 8 × 7 × 6 × 5 × 4 × 3 × 2 × 1. This quantity is written 8! and is termed "eight factorial." Different orderings of objects in a group are called "permutations."

We can mentally evaluate 8! as 40,320. So our desired probability is 1/40,320. One interpretation of this answer is that if you witnessed 40,320 horse races, you would "on the average" witness one instance of the order of finish 1-2-3-4-5-6-7-8. If you went to the horse races every day, 365 days a year, and witnessed ten races each day, it would take you over ten years to see 40,320 horse races.

The inquisitive reader may now wonder how factorials of respectable magnitude can be computed. After all, the factorial function grows immensely fast. 8! was itself quite large. 9! will be that times 9, and 10! will already be over one million. What if we needed to estimate something like 100!? How would we proceed?

Stirling's Formula

Here a remarkable theoretical result by Stirling comes to our rescue. Stirling provides us with an excellent approximation formula for computing large factorials. His result is as follows:

$$n! \approx (n^n)e^{-n} \sqrt{(2\pi n)}$$

where the symbol $\approx$ is used to denote "approximately equals."

We can use logarithms to estimate 100! by using Stirling's formula. Here is the method.

Step 1. Calculate n^n. Do this by taking the logarithm of n, multiplying this by n, and taking the antilogarithm. Taking n = 100, we have $\log(100) = 2$; multiplying this by 100 gives 200. Taking the antilog gives 10^{200}.

Step 2. Calculate e^{-n}. Here e is the base of natural logarithms, equal to 2.71828 .... Our method is to take the log to the base 10 of e, multiply this by –n, and take the antilog. Log e can be estimated as .434. This is a helpful number to remember. It can be estimated, however, as about 72% of the way from log(2) to log(3).

Multiplying $.434 \times -100$ gives –43.4. This is the log of e^{-n}. To take the antilog, note that the characteristic is –44 and the mantissa is .6. Since $\log(4) = .602$, we can estimate the antilog of .6 as 4. This gives 4×10^{-44} as an approximation for e^{-n}.

Step 3. Calculate $\sqrt{(2\pi n)}$. Here we can estimate 2π as about 6.28, which, multiplied by 100, gives 628. We can take the square root by linear interpolation, with $25^2 = 625$ and $26^2 = 676$. So the square root of 628 is about $3/51$ of the way from 25 to 26, or about 25.06.

Step 4. Perform the final multiplication.

$$(10^{200})(4 \times 10^{-44})(25.06)$$

This is about 100.24×10^{156}, or 1.0024×10^{158}. The CRC standard math tables list the value of 100! as 9.33×10^{157}.

Poker Hand Probabilities

An interesting class of event counting problems comes from poker. We can calculate the probability of being dealt certain poker hands in five-card stud. In this game, you are dealt five cards only. There are no wild cards, nor are there any opportunities to exchange cards.

In order to analyze poker-related problems, we need to introduce the concept of a combination. A combination is a way of selecting a certain number of objects from a larger group. Order is not important. Each possible five-card poker hand is a combination. It is a way of selecting five objects from a group of fifty-two.

Mathematical theory tells us that the number of ways of selecting r objects from a group of n is $n!/r!(n-r)!$. This is symbolically represented as $\binom{n}{r}$.

We can use this theory to calculate the probabilities of being dealt various poker hands. Recalling the principles of event counting, for each type of poker hand our desired probability will be the number of equally likely favorable outcomes divided by the total number of outcomes. The total number of outcomes is just $\binom{52}{5}$, the number of ways of selecting five cards from a group of fifty-two, where order of selection is not important. This is evaluated as:

$$52!/(5!)(47!) = (52)(51)(50)(49)(48)/(5)(4)(3)(2)(1) =$$
$$(52)(51)(5)(49)(4)$$

Stop! Don't reach for that calculator! By intelligently regrouping these terms and employing the techniques of Chapter 3, you can do this mentally. You really can. Take your time and work through it. It's not a race. If you get the right answer, I think you can proudly step forth and proclaim yourself among the wise of mental math wizardom. When you have your answer, continue reading, and we can compare methods and answers.

Here, I would regroup terms in the order $52 \times (51 \times 49) \times (5 \times 4)$. 51×49 is a nice problem by the method of squares. It is just $(50 + 1)(50 - 1)$, or $50^2 - 1^2 = 2{,}499$. Now we have $52 \times 2{,}499 \times 20$.

Multiplying by 20 is always easy, so I would save that until last. I would compute $52 \times 2{,}499$ by the Upper Roundoff method, breaking it up as $52 \times 2{,}500 - 52$. $52 \times 2{,}500 = 130{,}000$ (one way to do this quickly is to look at 2,500 as $.25 \times 10{,}000$). Then $52 \times 2{,}499 = 130{,}000 - 52 = 129{,}948$. We are left with $129{,}948 \times 20$. We double 129,948 and add a 0 to get the final answer of 2,598,960.

We will use this as our total number of outcomes. For various types of hands, we can calculate the number of favorable outcomes and then divide by the total that we have just calculated. If you want to stay in a machine-free environment, I think you can be allowed to approximate 2,598,960 as 2.6 million.

As a start, we can compute the number of ways of being dealt a flush. This is five cards of the same suit, which don't comprise a straight flush or a royal flush.

We start by selecting the suit in which the flush lies, which can be done in four ways. Next we must select five cards of the thirteen in the suit to comprise the flush. This can be done in $\binom{13}{5}$, or 1,287 ways. That gives us so far $4 \times 1,287 = 5,148$. But we must still subtract the number of straight flushes or royal flushes, which are separate hands. There are forty of these to subtract (see Table 14-1). That leaves $5,148 - 40 = 5,108$. Our probability is then 5,108/ (2.6 million) — about 1 in 500.

As a second, less exciting but more difficult example, we can compute the number of ways of being dealt an ordinary pair. There are several ways of arriving at the same answer to this problem. I will present one of them here.

A hand containing one pair consists of four denominations in all (for example, a hand with a pair of aces, a queen, a five, and a three contains aces, queens, fives, and threes). So we can start with $\binom{13}{4}$ ways of selecting these four denominations. Of these four, one of them is the special one, which has the pair. This special denomination is chosen in $\binom{4}{1}$ ways. Of the four cards in the special denomination, a pair is chosen in $\binom{4}{2}$ ways. Finally, the three remaining cards that make up the hand can be chosen in 4^3 ways, remembering that their denominations have already been determined. Putting it all together we get:

$$\binom{13}{4} \binom{4}{1} \binom{4}{2} 4^3 = 1,098,240$$

We can approximate the probability of being dealt this hand by performing the division 1.1 / 2.6. This is about .42, as the reader can easily verify.

Table 14-1 summarizes the calculations for all poker hands. Readers may want to use it to test their understanding of combinations.

SEQUENTIAL EVENTS

This category of problems differs from "Event Counting" since we no longer assume that outcomes are equally likely. As events happen in sequence, we allow for the possibility that outcomes of past events can affect outcomes of future events. If this is true, we say that the events are dependent.

The concept of conditional probability is key in working with dependent events. We speak symbolically of $Pr(B|A)$ to mean the probability that B occurs given that A has occurred. This is referred to as a conditional probability. We can now compute the probability of both A and B occurring as $Pr(A)Pr(B|A)$.

TABLE 14-1. Poker hand probabilities.

Poker Hand	Combinations	Favorable Outcomes	Approximate Probability
Pair	$\binom{13}{4}\binom{4}{1}\binom{4}{2}\,4^3$	1,098,240	.42
2 Pairs	$\binom{13}{2}\binom{3}{2}\binom{4}{2}\binom{4}{2}\,4$	123,552	.05
3 of a Kind	$\binom{13}{3}\binom{4}{1}\binom{4}{3}\,4^2$	54,912	1 in 47
Straight	$10(4^5 - 4)$	10,200	1 in 250
Flush	$\binom{4}{1}\binom{13}{5} - 40$	5,108	1 in 500
Full House	$\binom{13}{2}\binom{4}{1}\binom{4}{3}\binom{4}{2}$	3,744	1 in 700
4 of a Kind	$\binom{13}{2}\binom{4}{1}\binom{4}{4}\,4$	624	1 in 4,000
Straight Flush	$10\binom{4}{1} - 4$	36	1 in 70,000
Royal Flush	4	4	1 in 649,740

Draw Poker Conditional Probability

Numerous examples of conditional probability come from the game of draw poker. Here, five cards are dealt, then players may exchange no, one, two, or three cards in an attempt to improve their hand.

Suppose your hand consists of four cards of the same suit and one "loner." In poker talk, you are said to hold a "four-flush." Now you want to discard the loner in the hope of getting a flush. What are your chances? Well, there are fifty-two cards in the deck. Five of them were in your original hand, leaving forty-seven possibilities from which to choose. Your favorable outcomes amount to nine possibilities, since there are 13 − 4 = 9 cards of your desired suit remaining. So, by simple division, the probability is 9/47, or about .19.

Next we can calculate the probability of filling a "three-flush," i.e., holding three cards of a suit, drawing two cards and filling the flush. We need to compute:

Pr(First card is favorable) ×
 Pr(Second card is favorable|First card is favorable)

The reader can verify the answer of (10/47)(9/46). This is 90/2162, or about 1 in 24.

A more advanced problem is if you hold three of a kind and

discard two cards in the hope of getting either a full house or four of a kind. What are your chances?

To get a full house, your first card must match any of twelve remaining denominations, and your second card must match your first card. Remember your two discards! In the unfortunate case that your first card matches one of your two discards, your chances of a hit on the second card decrease. Taking these considerations into account, we can adopt the following notation to aid us in calculating the probability of hitting the full house:

A: The event that the first card does not match a discard.
B: The event that the first card matches a discard.
C: The event that the second card matches the first card.

(A and B implicitly assume that the first card also does not match the three of a kind, as that would make four of a kind.)

We wish to compute:

$$Pr(A)Pr(C|A) + Pr(B)Pr(C|B)$$

We can evaluate these four probabilities individually:

$$Pr(A) = 40/47$$
$$Pr(B) = 6/47$$
$$Pr(C|A) = 3/46$$
$$Pr(C|B) = 2/46 = 1/23$$

Readers should verify the above probabilities to test their understanding. Now we can plug the numbers into our equation to get:

$$(40/47)(3/46) + (6/47)(1/23) = (120/2,162) + (6/1081) = \text{about } .059.$$

This is the probability of hitting a full house. The probability of hitting four of a kind is easier to compute. If the first card hits with probability $1/47$, the second card can be anything. If the first card misses with probability $46/47$, then the second card must hit with probability $1/46$. The total probability is then:

$$1/47 + (46/47)(1/46) = 1/47 + 1/47 = 2/47 = \text{about } .043.$$

Finally, the total probability of improving your hand is $.059 + .043 = .102$.

Craps Probability

An interesting problem in sequential events is to analyze the game of casino craps. The rules of this game are as follows:

1. The player rolls two dice, noting the total.

2. If the player's roll totals 7 or 11, he wins at once.

3. If the player's roll totals 2, 3, or 12, he loses at once.

4. If the player's roll totals 4, 5, 6, 8, 9, or 10, the value of the roll is termed the "point." The player continues to roll. The game continues until the player rolls either the point or a 7. If the player rolls the point first, he wins. If the player rolls a 7 first, he loses.

We can mathematically pose the question, "What is the probability of winning at craps?"

As we will see, the problem is difficult. But a good start is to use event counting to get the probabilities of various first rolls. We actually have a start on this from an earlier example in the "Event Counting" section of this chapter. We can finish this off and place the results in table form.

Now adopt the following notation:

W: The event of winning.

n: The event of rolling a value of n on the first roll, where n can range from 2 to 12.

We can write:

$$Pr(W) = Pr(7) + Pr(11) + Pr(4)Pr(W|4) + Pr(5)Pr(W|5) + Pr(6)Pr(W|6) + Pr(8)Pr(W|8) + Pr(9)Pr(W|9) + Pr(10)Pr(W|10)$$

The lengthy expression can be simplified by noting the problem's symmetry. From Table 14-2, we can infer that $Pr(4) = Pr(10)$, $Pr(5) = Pr(9)$, and $Pr(6) = Pr(8)$. It is also obviously true that $Pr(W|4) = Pr(W|10)$, $Pr(W|5) = Pr(W|9)$, and $Pr(W|6) = Pr(W|8)$. So we can rewrite the lengthy expression as:

$$Pr(W) = Pr(7) + Pr(11) + 2[Pr(4)Pr(W|4) + Pr(5)Pr(W|5) + Pr(6)Pr(W|6)]$$

To evaluate this expression, all we need to compute are the values $Pr(W|4)$, $Pr(W|5)$, and $Pr(W|6)$. Everything else is known directly from Table 14-2.

TABLE 14-2. Dice-throwing probabilities.		
Total	Favorable Outcomes	Probability
2	1	1/36
3	2	1/18
4	3	1/12
5	4	1/9
6	5	5/36
7	6	1/6
8	5	5/36
9	4	1/9
10	3	1/12
11	2	1/18
12	1	1/36

Let's start by computing $Pr(W|6)$. Here we are assuming that the initial roll of the game was a 6. Now we must roll another 6 before rolling a 7. We must account for the following possibilities:

1. A 6 is rolled on the very next roll.
2. A non-6 or a 7 is rolled followed by a 6.
3. A non-6 or 7 is rolled twice, followed by a 6.
4. A non-6 or 7 is rolled three times, followed by a 6.

Etcetera, ad infinitum.

Infinite Series

The problem introduces us to an interesting topic of mathematics called infinite series. The number of terms needed to evaluate $Pr(W|6)$ is infinite. However, the terms become increasingly smaller and approach (although never equal) 0. But it is possible to find the sum of such a series, even though the sum of an infinite number of terms is difficult to visualize conceptually.

As an example, consider the infinite series $1 + (\frac{1}{2}) + (\frac{1}{4}) + (\frac{1}{8})$ + . . . where each term is half of its predecessor. Intuitively, the sum of this series is 2, because this sum approaches 2 as the number of terms gets larger and larger. The sum of an infinite series is not always this obvious. However, a special technique can be employed for evaluating a so-called "geometric series," in which each term is a constant multiple of its predecessor, and that multiple is less than one.

Consider the general form of the geometric infinite series:

$$S = 1 + q + q^2 + q^3 + \ldots$$

We must have $|q| < 1$ for the series to converge. Otherwise its sum will be infinite. Now multiple both sides of the above relation by q to obtain:

$$qS = q + q^2 + q^3 + \ldots$$

Notice that the right hand sides of the two relations are identical except for the "1" that appears in the first equation. Noticing this, we can write:

$$S - qS = 1, \text{ or } S = 1/(1 - q) \qquad \text{(Equation 14-1)}$$

Here S is the sum of the infinite series, and the result of Equation 14-1 provides us with a simple way of computing the sum of a general geometric infinite series in terms of the constant multiple.

We can now use this theory to evaluate $Pr(W|6)$. We can begin by recording the following relationships:

Pr(rolling a 6 on the next roll) = 5/36 — from Table 14-2
Pr(rolling a non-6 or 7 on any roll) = 1 – (1/6) –
$\qquad\qquad\qquad$ (5/36) = 25/36
Pr(rolling a non-6 or 7 followed by a 6) = (25/36)(5/36)
Pr(rolling a non-6 or 7 twice in a row followed by a 6) =
$\qquad\qquad\qquad$ $(25/36)^2 (5/36)$
Pr(rolling a non-6 or 7 r times in a row followed by a 6) =
$\qquad\qquad\qquad$ $(25/36)^r (5/36)$

The first few terms of the infinite series can now be written:

$$(5/36) + (25/36)(5/36) + (25/36)^2(5/36) + (25/36)^3(5/36) + \ldots$$

We can factor out 5/36 to obtain:

$$(5/36)[1 + (25/36) + (25/36)^2 + (25/36)^3 + \ldots]$$

Recognizing the terms in brackets as the infinite geometric series with q = 25/36, we can write its sum quickly as 36/11 by using Equation 14-1. Then our sum is (5/36)(36/11) = 5/11. This is $Pr(W|6)$.

In identical fashion, we can compute $Pr(W|4)$ and $Pr(W|5)$. The results are laid out in Table 14-3.

TABLE 14-3. Probabilities of winning your point in craps.	
Point	Probability
4 or 10	1/3
5 or 9	2/5
6 or 8	5/11

Finally, we can set $Pr(W|4) = 1/3$, $Pr(W|5) = 2/5$, and $Pr(W|6) = 5/11$ and calculate the probability of winning at craps, using the previously developed relationship:

$$Pr(W) = Pr(7) + Pr(11) + 2[Pr(4)Pr(W|4) + Pr(5)Pr(W|5) + Pr(6)Pr(W|6)]$$

$$Pr(W) = (1/6) + (1/18) + 2[(1/12)(1/3) + (1/9)(2/5) + (5/36)(5/11)]$$

Adding all this up, using a common denominator of 990 (18 × 11 × 5), we get 488/990 or 244/495 — just a touch less than ½.

PROBABILISTIC DECISION-MAKING

An important and interesting application of probability theory is decision-making and strategy formulation. We can imagine a decision to be made. There are any number of choices (strategies), from which we must select one. For each possible strategy, there exist several possible outcomes, each occurring with some probability. With each outcome is associated a certain profit or loss, which can be expressed as a numeric quantity. What should we do? What is our best strategy?

Central to this question is the notion of expected value. In words, this is the average profit or loss we would realize if we made the same decision in the same circumstances very many times. Mathematically, we compute expected value by adding up all the profits (with losses denoted as negative profits) times their respective probabilities. That gives us our expected profit for that strategy. Then, we can compare all the expected profits for all the different strategies and select the one that has the highest.

Choosing the Best Risk

Example 1. We are standing in a Las Vegas casino by the craps table. Our decision is whether or not to play craps. Our first choice is not to play, in which case we walk away with a profit of 0. Our second choice is to play. Here we have a profit of +1 (the reader may decide the units) with probability 244/495, and a profit of –1 with probability 251/495. Our expected profit if we play is 1(244/495) – 1(251/495) = –7/495. Strategy 1 gives us a higher expected profit, so we walk away and don't play.

Example 2. We are playing draw poker, holding a four-flush. There is 3 dollars in the pot, which we will most assuredly win if we hit our flush. It will cost us 50 cents to stay in the game and draw our one card. If we fold, our profit is 0. (We must view our prior contributions to the pot as no longer ours.) If we stay, we earn a profit of +3 with probability .19, and a profit of –.5 with probability .81. Our expected profit if we stay is 3(.19) – .5(.81) = .57 – .41 = .16. So we select the second choice (staying in the game), based on the higher expected profit. Warning: we did assume that, if we hit the flush, we would win the pot with probability 1.0. This is only an approximation, and we should take into account our suspicions about our competitors' holdings.

Baseball Strategy

More interesting and complicated examples of this idea come from sports events. We can illustrate with a hypothetical scenario from baseball.

Suppose the New York Mets are at bat in a tie baseball game that has been a closely fought pitchers' duel. Neither pitcher shows signs of tiring. There is one out with a runner on second base. It is the pitcher's turn at bat, and he will bat. What is the probability that the New York Mets will score a run this inning?

The correct answer to this question is, "It depends." There are many different strategies that the New York Mets can select to try to score their run. For the purpose of getting a reasonable handle on this problem and at the same time be able to tackle it in a machine-free way, we will analyze four different strategies:

Strategy 1. Pitcher swings away, trying to get a base hit. The lead-off batter, who is up next, tries to do the same.

Strategy 2. Runner on second attempts to steal third. If he is successful, the pitcher (still batting) will attempt to get him home via a suicide squeeze play.

Strategy 3. Runner on second tries to steal third. If he succeeds, the pitcher will swing away, trying to get either a base hit, a sacrifice fly, or a run-scoring ground ball.

Strategy 4. Pitcher bunts, trying to advance the runner to third. Lead-off batter, up next, swings away.

We will mathematically analyze each of these four strategies in turn.

Strategy One. If either the pitcher or the lead-off batter gets a run-scoring base hit, the run will score. We will take .190 as the pitcher's batting average (at the time of writing this book, the Mets' pitchers are fairly good hitters), and .270 as the lead-off hitter's batting average. The probability of a run-scoring base hit is slightly less than the batting average (some base hits cannot score a run from second base). We will use .150 (for the pitcher) and .230 (for the lead-off man) as probabilities of run-scoring base hits.

The probability that neither gets a run-scoring hit is $(1 - .150)(1 - .230) = .85 \times .77 =$ about .65. Thus, the probability of scoring a run is $1 - .65 = .35$.

Strategy Two. We will assume that the runner on second can succeed in stealing third with probability .25 (at the time of this book's writing, the New York Mets' seventh and eighth batters are not base-stealing threats). We will assume that the probability of a successful suicide squeeze play is .5. The probability that both these events will happen is $.25 \times .5 = .125$, which is the probability of scoring a run.

Strategy Three. We will assume, as in strategy two, that the runner on second can successfully steal third with probability .25. If he succeeds, then the pitcher can bring him home with either a hit, a sacrifice fly, or a ground ball. The probability of the pitcher having such an at-bat is considerably greater than his batting average. We will use .55 as this probability, based on the current New York Mets' excellent hitting pitchers.

Verbally, the runner on second must steal third (.25) and, in addition, either the pitcher must drive him home (.55), or the lead-off batter must get a hit (.27). Mathematically we have (.25)

$[1 - (.45)(.73)] = .25(1 - .33) = .25 \times .67 = .17$, which is the probability of scoring a run.

Strategy Four. We will assume that the probability of a successful sacrifice is .6 (in which the runner advances), and the probability of an unsuccessful sacrifice is .4. To score a run, we need both a successful sacrifice and a hit by the lead-off batter. The probability of both these events occurring is $.6 \times .270 = .16$, which is the probability of scoring a run.

Based on this analysis, we conclude that the best strategy, by a good margin, is strategy one, with a corresponding run-producing probability of .35.

Our analysis, though reasonable, certainly does not encompass all possibilities. The reader may have caught several omissions. Walks were never taken into account. Fielding errors were ignored, along with double play possibilities and many other scenarios. (For example, in strategy two, after a failed suicide squeeze the inning is not yet over.) We wanted to count the main possibilities, the things that would be most likely to happen. We did this for two reasons:

1. We want to be able to do the calculating quickly and without carrying some machine around.
2. The roughness of our data does not justify extensive analytical depth.

The important point in this example was the method. We started with a number of different possible strategies. For each strategy, we define the outcomes and the probabilities of reaching each outcome. Each outcome has a value associated with it. We then use the information to select the strategy that yields the highest expected value.

The technique has almost unlimited application. Football and other sports strategy decisions provide one area. Business-world decision-making would certainly benefit from this approach, which requires strong up-front thinking, but yields crisp, clean results. Decisions in normal day-to-day life may provide even more opportunities to use such a technique. Should I change jobs? Should I listen to my doctor's advice? How hard should I study chemistry next year? How many of us think through these decisions by considering the weights of all the possible consequences, and the likelihoods of each?

We will conclude this chapter with two interesting problems in probability.

VOTING BOOTH PROBABILITIES

Have you ever gone to the voting booth and wondered if your time and energy were being wasted? "There are thousands of people voting on this thing," you might have said. "My vote isn't going to matter."

Guess again. Your vote is more important than you realize. Mathematically, we can ask the following question: Given an election with n voters, with n an even number and yourself being the $(n+1)$-th, what is the probability that the n voters will split exactly in half, and you will cast the deciding vote? (Note: If the number of voters is odd, the probability will be for you to cast the tying vote. Throughout the following analysis, for simplicity and drama, we will assume an even number of voters.)

The theory that we will need is a simple formula you can probably derive for yourself if you think about it. The formula is as follows: If an experiment has only two outcomes, success with probability p and failure with probability $(1-p)$, then the probability of exactly r successes in t trials is:

$$\binom{t}{r} p^r (1-p)^{t-r}$$

Let's say we have a close election, where support for each side is roughly equal. Mathematically, we would say that a person selected randomly from the voting population would select either alternative with probability $\frac{1}{2}$. Then, in our formula we have p = .5. We can also set t = n (the number of people, other than yourself, voting), and r = n/2. This gives us $\binom{n}{n/2}(1/2)^n$. We need to evaluate this. That is our answer.

But recall that $\binom{n}{n/2} = n!/[(n/2)!]^2$. If n and n/2 are big numbers, perhaps in the thousands or millions, then how can we evaluate n! and $(n/2)!$!? The answer is Stirling's approximation formula, from which we have $n! = n^n e^{-n} \sqrt{2\pi n}$ and $(n/2)! = (n/2)^{n/2} e^{-n} \sqrt{\pi n}$.

We can plug all this into our formula to get:

$$(\tfrac{1}{2})^n n^n e^{-n} \sqrt{(2\pi n)} / \{[(n/2)^{n/2}]^2 [e^{-n/2}]^2 [\sqrt{(2\pi n)} / 2]^2\}$$

Amazingly, almost all of this cancels out, as the reader can verify. The final answer, after cancellation, is $\sqrt{2/n\pi}$, or approximately $1/1.25\sqrt{n}$.

TABLE 14-4. Probability of casting the deciding vote in various situations.

Group/Situation	No. of Voters	Probability of Swinging the Vote
Group of friends	8	.28
Classroom election	40	.12
United States Senate	100	1 in 12
High school election	1,500	1 in 48
Small local election	7,000	1 in 100
Large local election	60,000	1 in 300
State of Maine election	600,000	1 in 960
State of California election	9,000,000	1 in 3750

We can apply this result to some practical voting circumstances that the reader may encounter. Table 14-4 lists for various situations the probability that your vote will decide the issue.

From Table 14-4, it is still not likely that your vote will swing a big election. But your chances of doing so are much higher than you might have thought.

Noteworthy, however, is that we have assumed a close election, with our parameter p = .5. If p were not .5, our results would be quite different, and, in a large election, the chances of casting the deciding vote would be close to 0. But, given a close election, your chances of affecting the result are not bad. If you live in the state of Maine, your chances of swinging the next statewide close election are not much worse than your chances of being dealt a full house in your next poker hand. If you live in California, your chances of swinging the next statewide election are much better than your chances of winning the next state lottery.

FORTUNETELLING OR PROBABILITY?

When you read in the paper about psychics or prophets predicting dire events, are you scared? If you are like most people, you might be open-minded about psychics and their ability to look into the future. You might be influenced in part by a sensationalist media, which publicizes successful predictions and downplays unsuccessful ones.

In today's society, as in all societies of the past, there are hordes of people claiming to have some vision of future events. Some are harmless fortunetellers, palm readers, and writers of astrology columns in newspapers. Others claim to possess a gift from God and proceed to make huge amounts of money based on this claim.

Is it really possible to foretell the future? Is there really such a thing as a legitimate psychic? These questions are far beyond the scope of this book. But, through the mathematics of probability theory, we can calculate the likelihood of predicting some future event by chance guessing.

First, we need to choose some future event that, at this time, cannot be predicted by science. To many Californians, the date of the next big quake (Richter 7.5 or greater) is a significant concern, and it is also a favorite target for psychics.

There will be many predictions of this event. Many people will enter more than one prediction in the mad dash to fame and fortune that will go to the correct predictor. For the purposes of this problem, let's suppose that they are all guessing. What is the probability that at least one of them will get lucky? What is the probability that at least one of them will nail it exactly — the exact date and year of the next big quake?

This problem differs significantly from all others in this chapter. Until now, all random variables considered have taken on discrete values (e.g., poker hands, totals rolled on dice, results of a baseball at-bat). Unlike those previous random variables, the time of the next earthquake in California is a random variable that can take on a continuum of values. The implications of this difference are significant, and a small introduction to the ideas of integral calculus is necessary as background for this problem.

A Little Calculus

The central problem of integral calculus can be stated as follows: Given a function $f(x)$, find the area under the curve determined by $f(x)$ between some limits x_1 and x_2. See Figure 14-1.

We can actually calculate the area under the curve by dividing the shaded region into many skinny rectangles, where the height of each rectangle is the height of the curve above the x-axis. We can use the concept of limits in calculus to figure out the sum of the rectangular areas as the rectangles become infinitesimally skinny.

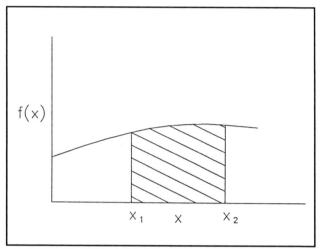

FIGURE 14-1. *Area under a curve.*

This is called "the integral of f(x) from x_1 to x_2" and is written $\int_{x_1}^{x_2}$ f(x)dx. To evaluate this quantity, we do the following:

1. Find the function whose derivative is f(x). Derivatives were originally encountered in Chapter 7.
2. Evaluate this new function (call it F(x)) at x_1 and at x_2, then compute the difference $F(x_2) - F(x_1)$. (See Appendix B for an explanation of the theory behind this method.)

As a quick example of this technique we can calculate the area of the shaded trapezoidal region in Figure 14-2. It is bounded by the curve y = mx + b and the two vertical lines x = x_1 and x = x_2.

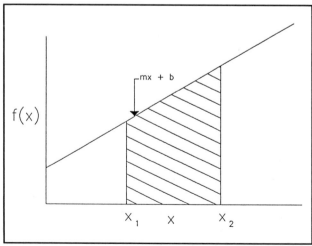

FIGURE 14-2. *Find the area of the trapezoidal region.*

By our theory, we can write $\int_{x_1}^{x_2}$ (mx + b)dx as an expression for the area. We can evaluate this integral by the following method:

Step 1. Find the function whose derivative is mx+b. The advanced reader will see quickly that this is $(m/2)x^2$ + bx.

Step 2. Calculate the difference (F(x₂) – F(x₁)), where F(x) denotes $(m/2)x^2$ + bx. This difference is $(m/2)x_2^2$ + bx₂ – $(m/2)x_1^2$ – bx₁. This is our area. This can be rearranged algebraically to give:

$$(x_2 - x_1)^x \, [(mx_1 + b) + (mx_2 + b)] \, / \, 2$$

The reader may recognize this as the more familiar formula for the area of a trapezoid.

When working with a random variable that can have a continuum of values (for example, the time until the next big California quake), the concept of a probability density function is key. See Figure 14-3. The total area under this curve is 1, to represent the total probability of all outcomes possible. The probability that the random variable x lies in the interval (x₁,x₂) is $\int_{x_1}^{x_2}$ f(x)dx. This is the area of the shaded region in the figure.

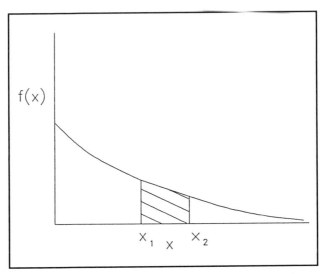

FIGURE 14-3. *Exponential probability density function.*

Earthquakes belong to a class of phenomena whose behavior can be approximately modeled by using a probability density function of the form $\lambda e^{-\lambda x}$. This is called the exponential probability density function. Figure 14-3 is a sketch of this function. The random variable x represents the time from the present to the next occurrence of the event. (See Appendix C for a derivation of the exponential probability density function.)

The advanced reader may want to verify that the total area under the curve is 1, i.e., that $\int_0^\infty \lambda e^{-\lambda x} dx = 1$. The advanced reader may also want to verify that the mean time to the next event is $1/\lambda$. This can be done by evaluating the integral $\int_0^\infty \lambda x e^{-\lambda x} dx$.

The main postulate behind the exponential distribution is that it is memoryless. Whether the last event occurred five centuries ago or three seconds ago, the probability density function for the time to wait until the next event is still $\lambda e^{-\lambda x}$. (Here earthquake scientists may point out that earthquake behavior is only memoryless to an approximation. In fact, the occurrence of a quake may increase the likelihood of more quakes to follow. But we are using the exponential here only as an approximation for large quakes, not for smaller aftershock or foreshock behavior.)

We will assume that, on the average, a major quake will hit California once every sixty years. Then we will use the exponential probability density function with $1/\lambda = 60$ years or 21,900 days. So $\lambda = 1/21{,}900$.

We will assume that the guesses follow the same pattern; that is they are distributed exponentially with parameter $\lambda = 1/21{,}900$. The likelihood of a correct guess is pictorially depicted in Figure 14-4.

In Figure 14-4, let us suppose the quake happens at some point in time Q. Guesses are represented by tiny strips with widths equal to 1 day each. If a guess happens to envelop Q, then that guess scores a hit.

You may see one way of doing this problem. We could try to add the areas associated with all the guesses, and calculate the area under the curve that the guesses will cover. This is difficult since guesses may overlap each other. A far more tractable method is to analyze the probability distribution of the difference of random variables, the quake time and the guess.

We can imagine the following procedure:

1. Select a random variable x to represent the quake time.
2. Select a random variable y to represent the guess.
3. Calculate the difference $(x - y)$. If this difference is between $-(\frac{1}{2})$ and $\frac{1}{2}$ (units of days), then the guess is sufficiently close to envelop the quake time.

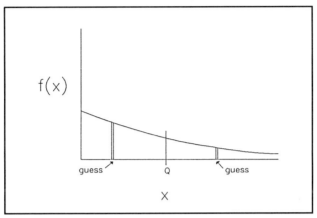

FIGURE 14-4. *Guessing the date of the next quake.*

We need to find the probability density function of $(x - y)$. We assume both x and y are exponentially distributed random variables with parameter $\lambda = 1/21{,}900$. The probability density function for this difference is sketched in Figure 14-5.

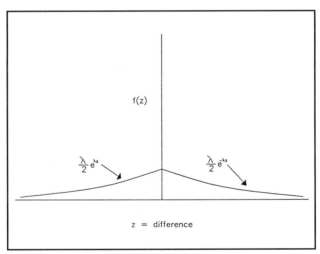

FIGURE 14-5. *Probability density function for the difference of two exponentially distributed random variables, each with parameter λ.*

Here $z = x - y$ represents the random variable that is the difference between the quake time and the guess. The advanced reader may verify this by evaluating the convolution integral $h(z) = \int_0^\infty f(x)f(z+x)dx$, where $f(x) = \lambda e^{-\lambda x}$.

Now we have everything we need to compute the probability that a single guess differs from the actual quake time by less than half a day. This is the probability that $-(1/2) < z < 1/2$, or:

$\int_{-1/2}^{1/2} h(z)dz$

$= \int_{-1/2}^{0}(\lambda/2) e^{\lambda z}dz + \int_{0}^{1/2}(\lambda/2) e^{-\lambda z}dz$

$= 2\int_{0}^{1/2} (\lambda/2) e^{-\lambda z}dz$, by making use of the problem's symmetry.

Now $\int e^{-\lambda z} = (-1/\lambda) e^{-\lambda z}$

So we have:

$2(\lambda/2)(-1/\lambda)e^{-\lambda z}|_{0}^{1/2}$

where the notation indicates we must evaluate $e^{-\lambda z}$ for both $z = \frac{1}{2}$ and $z = 0$, then take the difference. Evaluating further, we have:

$-(e^{-\lambda/2} - 1)$, since $e^0 = 1$.
$= 1 - e^{-\lambda/2}$
$= 1 - e^{-1/43800}$, substituting $\lambda = 1/21{,}900$

Now we have the probability of a single guess making a hit as $1 - e^{-1/43800}$. Since the hit probability plus the miss probability must equal 1, this means that the miss probability is $e^{-1/43800}$.

Let's suppose that there are 1,000 guesses made independently. The probability that they all miss is $e^{-1/43800}$ multiplied by itself 1,000 times. This gives $e^{-1000/43800} = .98$ as the probability of 1,000 misses. The probability of at least one hit is then $1 - .98 = .02$.

If the guessers don't guess the day, but guess the month, the identical logic can be used, with a change to the limits of integration (use -15.2 to $+15.2$ as limits instead of $-\frac{1}{2}$ to $+\frac{1}{2}$, 30.4 days per month on average). The answer to this, assuming again 1,000 guessers trying to pick the month and year, is amazingly .501, or slightly more than one-half. If the guessers only specify the season (e.g., "fall of 2045"), then the probability of at least one correct guess out of 1,000 rises to .878, and if the guessers specify only the year, it is virtually assured that at least one of them will hit.

PROBABILITIES IN LIFE

After reading this chapter, the reader may have the impression that probability is a useful tool for analyzing card games, craps, other gambling endeavors, and an occasional amusement. This is true. But probability is also more than this. It is much more.

Here are a few questions worth asking of probability theory's more human side:

What is the probability that you will still be alive twenty years from now? If your parents are both alive, what is the probability that they will both be alive ten years from now? What are the odds you will go to college and finish in the allotted time? Of your closest ten friends, what is the expected number of them who will still be your friends ten years from now?

Indeed, serious thought and research on the above questions can cause you to live life more fully, work harder to maintain your marriage, and cherish your friends and loved ones. Nothing is to be taken for granted in a world that contains so much uncertainty.

For behind all the intricate concepts and esoteric jargon, the study of probability springs from nothing more than the honest, forthright admission that we don't know how things will turn out. We will never know the future with certainty, and so we turn to probability theory for help.

And when this mighty science replies to our pleas, it speaks humbly. It doesn't offer brash predictions or impudent advice. It tells us only numbers, the simplest numbers, all between 0 and 1, that only express our degree of uncertainty in the future.

And if we listen to its gentle voice, it can change the way we live.

Chapter 15

Mathematical Trickery

Follow me, dear reader, and I will lead you on an interesting little excursion. First, I would like you to select three numbers between 1 and 9. Remember them. Now take the first number and double it. Now add 5. Multiply by 5. Recall the second number and add it. Multiply by 10. Now add the third number. Are you still with me? Do you have your answer?

If you tell me your answer, I will tell you your three numbers. If your answer was 723, your numbers were 4, 7, and 3. I can tell you just like that. What is the trick? Perhaps you want to take a few minutes to see if you can figure it out. After you have either discovered it or given up, read on.

Take your answer and subtract 250. That's the trick. Unless you have made a math mistake (which no readers of this book would ever do, of course), your three numbers should be sitting right there, in order, like ducks on a plate.

Why does it work? All it is is basic algebra. Let's call our three numbers x, y, and z. For the reader who is not fluent in algebra, Table 15-1 on the next page traces the algebraic steps of the problem.

The point is that 100x + 10y + z is just a three-digit quantity with the first number as the hundreds digit, the second number as the tens digit, and the third number as the units digit. There you have it. All you need to do is subtract 250 from the answer.

ANOTHER TRICK

All right, here's another one. Take a three-digit number. Remember it. Reverse the digits to get a second number. Subtract the smaller number from the bigger one to get a new number. Now reverse the digits again and add. Tell me how many digits are in your final

TABLE 15-1. Algebra behind "3 numbers" trick.

Step	Cumulative Algebraic Result
Take the first number.	x
Double it.	2x
Add 5.	2x + 5
Multiply by 5.	5(2x + 5) = 10x + 25
Add the second number.	10x + y + 25
Multiply by 10.	10(10x + y + 25) = 100x + 10y + 250
Add the third number.	100 x + 10y + z + 250

result, and I will tell you what that final result is. The reader may want to pause and reflect on this a minute. Can you see the trick? After you either figure it out, give up, or just want to see how it's done, read on.

There are only three answers that are possible — 0, 198, or 1,089. Let's see why. Express your number as 100h + 10t + u. Here h, t, and u are respectively the hundreds, tens, and units digits. Then the number with digits reversed is 100u + 10t + h. Let's assume that h is at least as large as u, so the original number is at least as large as itself reversed. (This assumption makes no difference whatsoever in our result.) Now we can perform the first subtraction:

$$(100h + 10t + u) - (h + 10t + 100u) = 99h - 99u = 99(h - u)$$

There are three possible results. They all depend on the relationship between the hundreds digit and the units digit of the original number:

1. These two numbers are equal. Then $99(h - u)$ will be 0, and this will be your answer.

2. These two numbers differ by 1. In this case $99(h - u) = 99(1) = 99$, and when you reverse the digits of 99 and add, you get 198. This will be your answer in this case.

3. These two numbers differ by anything from 2 through 9. In this case, the result of your subtraction, $99(h - u)$ will be one of the numbers in Table 15-2.

TABLE 15-2. Multiples of 99.	
(h - u)	99 (h - u)
2	198
3	297
4	396
5	495
6	594
7	693
8	792
9	891

But look! 2(99) and 9(99) are the same numbers with digits reversed. So are 3(99) and 8(99); so are 4(99) and 7(99); so are 5(99) and 6(99). What a coincidence! Whenever we take a number from this table, reverse its digits, and add them together, we will always get 11(99) = 1,089.

MODULAR ARITHMETIC

Here is another trick that is a bit more advanced. It depends on an area of mathematics called modular arithmetic, which we will explain during this trick's analysis.

Here is the trick. Pick a number from 1 to 1,000. Divide the number by 7, 11, and 13. Tell me only the three remainders, and I will tell you your number. For example, suppose your number was 200. As the reader can verify, 200/7 gives a remainder of 4, 200/11 gives a remainder of 2, and 200/13 gives a remainder of 5.

Now let's put you into the role of the trick performer. Someone tells you, "When I divided my number by 7 my remainder was 4, when I divided by 11 my remainder was 2, and when I divided by 13 my remainder was 5." So you are sitting there with 4, 2, and 5, and from that you have to deduce the answer as 200. How do you do it? Let's talk about it.

First notice that $7 \times 11 \times 13 = 1,001$. 7, 11, and 13 are also prime numbers, so they share no common factors. If you think about it intuitively, you should see that every number from 1 to 1,001 has unique values of the three remainders. This is true. Every number from 1 to 1,001 will produce a unique set of remainders, and to every set of three remainders there corresponds exactly one number between 1 and 1,001. But how do we go from knowing the remainders to getting the number?

Let's express our unknown number x and our three remainders of 4, 2, and 5 in terms of modular equations. We can write down the following relationship:

$$x = 4 \bmod 7 = 2 \bmod 11 = 5 \bmod 13$$

Here "mod" stands for "modulo." "x = 4 mod 7" means that when you divide x by 7 your remainder is 4. Another way to picture the modulo concept is by thinking of the way we tell time. Our hours are expressed as modulo 12. We count from 1 to 12, then start over again. In modular 12 arithmetic, we would use 0 instead of 12, but otherwise the comparison is the same. In modular 7 arithmetic, we count 0, 1, 2, 3, 4, 5, 6; 0, 1, 2, 3, 4, 5, 6; 0, 1, etc. The numbers equal to 4 modulo 7 are 4, 11, 18, 25, 32, etc.

With that background, we can continue to analyze the trick. The modular relationship really expresses three conditions. We will consider them one at a time, beginning with the first:

$$x = 4 \bmod 7$$

We ask the following question: How can we find a number that equals 4 modulo 7, 0 modulo 11, and 0 modulo 13? The idea behind this is the key to the trick. Why we want to do this will soon become clear.

Numbers that equal 0 in both modulo 11 and modulo 13 are multiples of 143. In Table 15-3 we list them and calculate their values in modulo 7.

Notice that all the values 0-6 for modulo 7 appear in the table. This is no accident. It is a natural consequence of the fact that 143 and 7 have no common factors.

When we see 858 in the table, a light bulb should flash in our minds. 858 is special because it equals 4 mod 7, 0 mod 11, and 0 mod 13. Let's remember 858, and proceed with the rest of the problem.

Our second condition is:

$$x = 2 \bmod 11$$

Here our question is: "What number equals 2 mod 11, 0 mod 7, and 0 mod 13?" We find out in exactly the same way, looking at multiples of 91. See Table 15-4.

TABLE 15-3. Multiples of 143 expressed in modulo 7.

Multiples of 143	Value in modulo 7
143	3
286	6
429	2
572	5
715	1
858	4
1001	0

TABLE 15-4. Multiples of 91 expressed in modulo 11.

Multiples of 91	Value in modulo 11
91	3
182	6
273	9
364	1
455	4
546	7
637	10
728	2
819	5
910	8
1001	0

Here 728 is our special number. Again, let's remember it and proceed with the last part of the problem.

Now we look at the last relationship:

x = 5 mod 13

We need a number that equals 5 modulo 13, 0 modulo 7, and 0 modulo 11. By now, the reader should understand the procedure at once. Table 15-5 contains what we need.

TABLE 15-5. Multiples of 77 expressed in modulo 13.

Multiples of 77	Value in modulo 13
77	12
154	11
231	10
308	9
385	8
462	7
539	6
616	5
693	4
770	3
847	2
924	1
1001	0

Here 616 is the magic number. Now we can remember our three numbers, 858, 728, and 616. If we add these three numbers together, we get 2,202. This number equals our answer modulo 1,001. So we subtract groups of 1,001 until we get a number that is less than 1,001. Then 2,202 – 1,001 = 1,201 and 1,201 – 1,001 = 200. And we have the right answer!

Why did this work? We can take our three special numbers, 858, 728, and 616, and summarize their properties as follows:

$858 = 4 \bmod 7 = 0 \bmod 11 = 0 \bmod 13$
$728 = 0 \bmod 7 = 2 \bmod 11 = 0 \bmod 13$
$616 = 0 \bmod 7 = 0 \bmod 11 = 5 \bmod 13$

Now the reader can see that when these numbers are added, the sum equals 4 modulo 7, 2 modulo 11, and 5 modulo 13. Those are precisely the properties of our answer. This doesn't mean that the sum is our answer. It just means that it has the same remainders as our answer. To find our answer, we must, as necessary, subtract groups of 1,001, an operation which preserves the values of the remainders.

What about doing this trick mentally? Perhaps the reader has noticed by inspection of Tables 15-3, 15-4, and 15-5 that the modulo values follow specific, predictable patterns. For example, from Table 15-3, 143 = 3 mod 7. From this, you can see that 2(143) = 2(3) mod 7, and 3(143) = 3(3) mod 7, etc. Thus, by counting by threes modulo 7, you can quickly derive the values in Table 15-3. In Table 15-4, the idea is to count by threes modulo 11, and in Table 15-5 the idea is to count by 12 modulo 13. This idea helps. But it's still hard.

There is another method, which requires simple memorization, and hence seems to lose some magic. But I will give it here. It depends on a theoretical result in modular arithmetic. The theoretical result says that if a = x mod m and b = y mod m, then ab = xy mod m. In words, multiplying two numbers gives a number with the same remainder as does multiplying their individual remainders together. Example: 10 = 1 mod 3, 20 = 2 mod 3, and 10(20) = 2 mod 3.

This result can help us to simplify our trick solution. Notice the following from Tables 15-3, 15-4, and 15-5:

From Table 15-3: 715 = 1 mod 7 = 0 mod 11 = 0 mod 13
From Table 15-4: 364 = 0 mod 7 = 1 mod 11 = 0 mod 13
From Table 15-5: 924 = 0 mod 7 = 0 mod 11 = 1 mod 13

Let's denote our three remainders as a, b, and c, and our answer as x. Then:

x = a mod 7 = b mod 11 = c mod 13.

Now we can use our theoretical result, along with our magic numbers 715, 364, and 924. Since x = a mod 7, x = 715a mod 7, since multiplying by 715 is equivalent to multiplying by 1. Similarly, x = 364b mod 11 and x = 924c mod 13. Notice now that 715a + 364b + 924c has the same properties as our desired number. So we can simply compute this quantity, then subtract groups of 1,001 until we have a number less than 1,000. For our problem, x = 200, a = 4, b = 2, c = 5. So 715(4) + 364(2) + 924(5) = 2,860 + 728 + 4,620 = 8,208. We subtract 8 groups of 1,001 to get 8,208 – 8,008 = 200 — again the right answer. Perhaps this method is a little easier for a mental application. All you have to do is remember 715, 364, and 924.

A PAWNSHOP PROBLEM

We will close this chapter with one last problem. It comes from the seedy, smoke-filled office of pawnbroker Chuck Plastic, who insists on using cash in all his transactions. Mr. Plastic does not charge sales tax for his merchandise.

Today Mr. Plastic has sold $5,000 worth of merchandise, purely from televisions and radios. He knows he has sold his televisions for $57 each and his radios for $32 each, but he doesn't remember how many of each he has sold. He's a bit sloppy with his paperwork. Can you help Mr. Plastic by telling him how many of each he has sold?

Perhaps the readers may want to try their hand at working this out before reading on.

This problem sounds deceptively simple. From algebra, we can write:

$$57T + 32R = 5,000$$

This one equation contains two unknowns. Such a system has an infinite number of solutions in real numbers. But here T and R must be non-negative integers. That restriction introduces a second constraint to the problem. An integer problem as this may have multiple solutions, one solution, or no solution.

A useful theorem applies here. In general an equation of the form $ax + by = n$ (where x and y are the unknowns and are non-negative integers) is guaranteed to have at least one solution if:

1. a and b are relatively prime; and
2. $n > ab - a - b$

We can apply this theorem to the numbers of Chuck Plastic's enterprise. We first note that 57 and 32 are relatively prime. We note second that $5,000 > 57 \times 32 - 57 - 32$. These two conditions guarantee in theory that we have a solution. So we have at least a partial check on the validity of the data supplied us by Mr. Plastic.

The problem can be solved in three steps as follows:

1. Solve the equation $57x + 32y = 1$ for x and y integers. Here, x and y may be negative, so I have distinguished them from the real non-negative solutions, which we call T and R. In general, of x and y, one will be positive and one negative.

2. Multiply x and y by 5,000 to get an integer solution to the equation 57x + 32y = 5,000. Either x or y will still be negative. That's okay.
3. Juggle things around so we can get a solution of non-negative integers from x and y.

Now let's apply these three steps to our problem.

Step 1. This is the hard part. First, since 57 and 32 are relatively prime (i.e., their greatest common divisor is 1), we are guaranteed by theory that an integer solution exists for 57x + 32y = 1. (An integer solution will exist for the equation ax + by = GCD(a,b), where GCD(a,b) denotes the greatest common divisor of a and b. The GCD of relatively prime numbers is 1.)

The concept of GCD is important to solving our problem. We know that the GCD of 57 and 32 is 1 by inspection. But we can apply Euclid's algorithm to 57 and 32 to find the GCD of these numbers, and in the process we can solve the equation 57x + 32y = 1. The explanation of this irony is that the important information provided by Euclid's algorithm is not the final result but the intermediate steps.

In words, Euclid's algorithm may be stated as follows: To find the GCD of two numbers, first divide the lower into the higher, obtaining a quotient and a remainder. Then do the same thing again, this time using the divisor and the remainder from the previous division. Repeat this process until seeing a 0 remainder. Then the next-to-last remainder is the GCD.

We can now apply this algorithm on 57 and 32 to give us the following set of results:

1. 57 = 32(1) + 25
2. 32 = 25(1) + 7
3. 25 = 7(3) + 4
4. 7 = 4(1) + 3
5. 4 = 3(1) + 1
6. 3 = 1(3) + 0

Here we see a 0 remainder and stop. The GCD is 1, and can be seen from the remainder in step 5.

Now the trick is to use backwards substitution, starting from step 5 and working our way backwards. The final goal is to solve for the remainder "1" of step 5 in terms of 57 and 32, the numbers of step 1.

Let's start by solving for "1" in step 5:

(*) $1 = 4 - 3(1)$

Now we use a cascading technique to go from step 5 upwards, always solving for remainders. So, solving for the remainder "3" in step 4 we have $3 = 7 - 4(1)$. Take the "3" thus solved for, and plug it into (*):

(*) $1 = 4 - [7 - 4(1)] = 4(2) - 7$

Continue by solving for the remainder "4" in step (3) to give $4 = 25 - 7(3)$. Now substitute this into (*):

(*) $1 = [25 - 7(3)]2 - 7 = 25(2) - 7(7)$

We continue by solving for "7" in step (2) and substituting into (*) to give the result $1 = 25(9) - 32(7)$. Finally, solve for "25" in step 1, and substitute to give:

(*) $1 = 57(9) - 32(16)$.
(*) $1 = 57(9) + 32(-16)$.

And we have our desired result.

Step 2. Multiply everything by 5,000 to get:

$57(45,000) + 32(-80,000) = 5,000$

Step 3. We need to juggle things around so everything is non-negative. Relax. This is easy. We must add something to –80,000 to make it positive and subtract something from 45,000, keeping it positive, while maintaining the total of 5,000.

We see that everything we add to –80,000 is multiplied by 32, and everything we subtract from 45,000 is multiplied by 57. The idea is to add groups of 57 to –80,000 until we make it positive, then subtract an equal number of groups of 32 from 45,000.

What is the required number of these magical groups? We only need to compute $80,000/57$ and then see that $57 \times 1,404 = 80,028$. So we need to add $57 \times 1,404$ to –80,000 and subtract $32 \times 1,404$ from 45,000. This gives us our first solution:

$57(72) + 32(28) = 5,000$ Solution 1

Other solutions can be found by the same idea (adding and subtracting groups of 57 and 32):

$$57(40) + 32(85) = 5,000 \qquad \text{Solution 2}$$
$$57(8) + 32(142) = 5,000 \qquad \text{Solution 3}$$

Armed with this information, we can now pay a visit to Mr. Plastic. The following conversation might ensue:

"Mr. Plastic, sir, I need more information to solve your problem. There is more than one possible solution."

"Humph," groans Plastic, rubbing his scraggly three-day beard. "Well, I'm sure I sold more radios than televisions."

"There are still two possibilities," you say to Plastic, after a glance at your three solutions. "I need more information."

"I sold at least ten televisions," says Plastic.

"I've got it! You've sold —"

"Wait a minute," interrupts Plastic, unfurling a crumpled dollar bill. "I guess I really pulled in $5,001 today."

Oh well. Have fun.

Notes

An excellent presentation of the theory of equations requiring integer solutions is given in *Introduction to Number Theory,* by Daniel Flath (New York: John Wiley and Sons, 1989). This book forms the basis for the theory used in developing a solution to Mr. Plastic's problem of this chapter.

Recreations in the Theory of Numbers, Second edition, by Albert H. Beiler (New York: Dover Publications Inc., 1964), is a fascinating collection of mathematical recreations in number theory. This book mentions the problem of divisions by 7, 11, and 13. The solution method that is given in this chapter is my own.

Chapter 16

Of Absolutely No Use

One nice thing about mathematics, particularly machine-free mathematics, is that it doesn't have to be useful to be fun. Some of the most fascinating problems in mathematics are those that have absolutely no useful purpose.

PRIME FACTORIZATION

For myself, I have always been fascinated by the problem of prime factorization. This type of problem, I suppose, fascinates me because there seems to be no apparent method that can be employed consistently. For example, how could you possibly find a method for deducing that 3,901 can be factored into 83 times 47? The question is interesting, but let's set it aside for a moment and talk about another one of my favorites.

I suppose it's not really a problem — just a wonder of algebra — but I've always been amazed by the simple truism that $a^2 - b^2$ = $(a + b)(a - b)$ for all values of a and b. This may mean nothing to you, the reader. You can multiply $(a + b)$ times $(a - b)$ in a straightforward algebraic manner and obtain the result $a^2 - b^2$.

But, look at the problem from the opposite end. Given the expression $a^2 - b^2$, how would you factor it? If you didn't know about the formula from algebra, how would you go about searching for it? To me, it's amazing to think that the difference of two squares can be factored in this way.

As you may have guessed, the two problems that fascinate me so much are closely related. In particular, the factorization formula of algebra can be used quite successfully to factor any number into primes. To appreciate this fact more, consider the following:

1. When factoring any number that is even, the number can be successively divided by 2 until an odd number results.

2. Any odd number, if it is factorable, is factorable by two odd numbers.

3. Two odd numbers differ from each other by an even number. Hence, they have some integer midpoint (call it a) and an even number difference (call it 2b). Their product can be written as (a + b)(a − b), or, yes, $a^2 − b^2$.

4. As a result of (3), we can factor an odd number by finding two squares whose difference is this number. This will give us the values of a and b, from which the factors can be deduced.

Now to formulate a method out of all this theory. Let's look at the problem of factoring 3,397. As preliminary steps, we note that this number cannot be divided evenly by 2, 3, 5, or 7.

We can continue by finding the nearest perfect square greater than or equal to 3,397. We note that 60^2 is 3,600, 59^2 is 3,600 − 119 = 3,481, and 58^2 = 3,481 − 117 = 3,364. So, we have 3,481 as our desired perfect square. The quantity 3,481 − 3,397 = 84 represents 59^2 − 3,397. We can write that 59^2 − 84 = 3,397. If 84 were a perfect square, we could now express 3,397 as the difference of two squares, and we would therefore have the desired factorization within sight. Since 84 is not a perfect square, we must continue our quest.

Since 59^2 − 3,397 does not give us a perfect square, we must ask if 60^2 − 3,397 gives us one. The difference 60^2 − 3,397 is really just 84 + 119, or 203. (Note that the difference between 60^2 − 3,397 and 59^2 − 3,397 is 60^2 − 59^2, or 119.)

But 203 is not a perfect square either. We can continue by computing 61^2 − 3,397 — adding 203 + 121 = 324, which we recognize as a perfect square (18^2). Thus we have 61^2 - 3,397 = 18^2, or that 61^2 − 18^2 = 3,397, which finally gives us 3,397 = (61 + 18)(61 − 18) = (79)(43).

Some Practice

We can try one more example to illustrate the method's computational shorthand approach. Let's find the factors, if any, of 8,777. First we note that this number cannot be divided by 2, 3, 5, or 7. We also note that the nearest perfect square exceeding 8,777 is 8,836 (94^2). We have the following:

$59 = 94^2 - 8,777$
$59 + 189 = \quad 248 = 95^2 - 8,777$
$248 + 191 = \quad 439 = 96^2 - 8,777$
$439 + 193 = \quad 632 = 97^2 - 8,777$
$632 + 195 = \quad 827 = 98^2 - 8,777$
$827 + 197 = 1,024 = 99^2 - 8,777$
$1,024$ is 32^2

Having reached a perfect square by this process, we now note that $99^2 - 32^2 = 8,777$. How did we get 99? Answer: the last number added was 197, which is 98 + 99. Our factors are then (99 + 32)(99 − 32), or 131 and 67.

What if a number is actually prime? How long must we continue this process before giving up? Since we check 2, 3, 5, and 7 before initiating the process, we know at the start of the algorithm that the numbers in question cannot be divided by a one-digit number.

The most lengthy computation will result when the two factors are farthest apart. The difference between the two factors is a maximum when the smaller factor is 11. If we denote the original number by n, the two factors will then be 11 and n/11. In this case, the factoring will be (a + b)(a − b), where:

$a = 11/2 + n/22$, and
$b = 11/2 + n/22 - 11$

In theory, we can discontinue the process and call the number a prime when our accumulated sum exceeds the quantity b^2, where b is defined as above. If the number we are attempting to factor is several digits long, the process could become extremely laborious. In practice, when the accumulated sum exceeds the original number itself, and no perfect square has yet been found, then there is an excellent chance that the number is prime.

PYTHAGOREAN TRIPLETS

A second problem-type along these lines is that of computing values of Pythagorean triplets. This is another challenging problem that is delightfully useless.

The problem of Pythagorean triplets is yet another instance in which the algebraic equation $a^2 - b^2 = (a + b)(a - b)$ provides the solution method.

As an example, let's consider a right triangle whose sides are of integer lengths and one of whose legs has a length of 51. What are the possible lengths of the other leg and of the hypotenuse?

Algebraically, we wish to find two other integers, say a and b, such that $51^2 + b^2 = a^2$, or that $a^2 - b^2 = 2{,}601$. We can factor this into $(a + b)(a - b) = 2{,}601$.

What are the possible values of a and b that will give a solution to our equation? One solution jumps out at us quickly. We can clearly set a − b equal to 1, in which case a + b would have to equal 2,601. In that case, we would have a = 1,301 and b = 1,300. This is a solution. We may check, in fact, that 51, 1,300 and 1,301 form a Pythagorean triplet.

There is no reason to stop at this first solution. In fact, we may choose a − b to have any value that is an integer factor of 2,601. The integer factors of 2,601 are the same as those of 51, since 2,601 is just 51^2. So our integer factors, other than 1, are then 3, 17, and 51. We may discount the factor 51, however, since it leads to the meaningless solution triplet of 1, 51, and 51. Therefore, we may choose 3 and 17 as possible values for the quantity a − b. We can tabularize our computations as follows:

a − b	a + b	a	b
3	867	435	432
17	153	85	68

And, in fact, we can show by squaring that there are three bona fide Pythagorean triplets associated with a leg of 51; and that these are: 51, 1,300, 1,301; 51, 432, 435; and 51, 68, 85. Note also that the triplet 51, 68, 85 is identical to the more familiar 3, 4, 5 triplet, since all the proportions are the same.

Some Practice

One more example may not be necessary, but it's always fun. Let's find the Pythagorean triplets associated with 44. This is a slightly different case from the last one, since 44, unlike 51, is an even number. This difference will become noteworthy shortly.

We start by squaring 44 to obtain 1,936. We next list the factors of 44 as 1, 2, 4, 11, and 22. The significance of 44 being an even number becomes apparent when we consider the first odd factor, namely 1. In this case, we have $(a + b)(a - b) = 1{,}936$, and we set a − b = 1. This requires that a + b = 1,936, or a = 968½ and b = 967½, two non-integer values.

In order for a and b to be integers, the two quantities (a + b) and (a − b) must either both be odd or both be even. Therefore, when we are dealing with an even number such as 44, we should choose only the even factors as possible values of a – b.

So, the factors of 44 that are usable to us are then 2, 4, and 22. We can assemble these factors in table form as in the previous example. This gives us the following:

a – b	a + b	a	b
2	968	485	483
4	484	244	240
22	88	55	33

And the corresponding triplets are 44, 483, 485; 44, 240, 244; and 33, 44, 55. The third triplet is yet another version of the common 3, 4, 5 triangle.

THE KING AND HIS CANNONBALLS PUZZLE

Perhaps it is best to close this book with a lasting gift — a puzzle posed mathematically for the reader to solve himself. It is also fitting that this problem is fun to solve without a computer. With a computer, the problem poses no challenge whatsoever, and consequently offers little as a reward for solving it. The problem is in the form of a story, entitled "The King and His Cannonballs."

There was once a king of an ancient country who undertook as a project the construction of cannonballs to bolster his military might. He also had a sense for the aesthetic and wished to arrange his cannonballs in certain patterns that would be pleasing to the eye.

So the king called in his royal mathematician.

"My mathematician," he said, tilting his chin deprecatingly. "I have a problem for you. I want to construct a number of cannonballs, and then arrange them in patterns on the royal lawn for all to behold. The first pattern I would like is to arrange all the cannonballs in a perfect square, in rows of equal numbers." He drew out a small sketch for the mathematician.

"So you want the total number of cannonballs to be a perfect square," said the mathematician.

"Quite so," said the king. "But now let me show you the second pattern that I wish to construct." The king sketched out a second picture and pointed to it.

"Here, I want to build a pyramid. I want one cannonball on the very top, four on the next-to-highest row, nine on the third-highest row, sixteen on the row below it, and so forth down to the bottom row."

"I see," said the mathematician. "So you also want your number of cannonballs to be the sum of squares between 1 and the height of the pyramid. There are then two requirements. Mathematically, we want to find a number n which is equal to m^2, and also equal to

$$\sum_{i=1}^{k} i^2$$

where n is the total number of cannonballs, m is the number of cannonballs on the side of your square, and k is the height of your pyramid. Your problem is interesting, especially since you want the answer to be an integer."

The king was annoyed at this last remark, which he considered unduly sarcastic. "Yes, you are right," he finally said. "What is the least number of cannonballs that I can have that will satisfy those conditions?"

The mathematician, who was a pacifist, didn't relish the idea of glorifying these cannonballs, which he saw as instruments of war.

"Zero," he said, after a moment's reflection.

The king was enraged. "Zero doesn't count, and don't get smart with me over a problem of so much importance. Don't pass off some trivial solution on me!"

"All right," said the mathematician, and thought about it a little further. "One."

The king was more enraged. "One doesn't count either. We are displaying a show of strength. We can't do that with one stupid cannonball! Give me a real answer or I'll have you thrown in chains!"

"All right," said the mathematician, hastily. "I'll work out your problem. Just let me go over and get my personal computer, and I'll whip up a quick little program. I'll have your solution in no time."

"Computer!" cried the king, now in hysterics. "You lunatic! This is ancient times! There aren't any computers around!"

"Okay," said the mathematician, and quietly began to work.

You're the mathematician. It's up to you to solve the king's cannonball problem. I can't keep you from using a computer, but I can tell you that it will be a lot less fun if you do.

Calculation of Derivatives

The formal definition of the derivative is as follows:

$$df(x)/dx = f'(x) = [\lim(\Delta x \to 0)] [f(x + \Delta x) - f(x) / \Delta x]$$

The rationale behind this definition is depicted in Figure A-1 below.

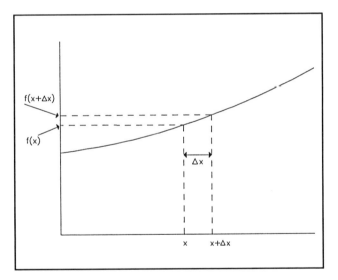

FIGURE A-1. *Calculation of the derivative as a limiting slope.*

As Δx is made smaller, the slope of the straight line approaches the slope of the curve at the point $(x,f(x))$. This slope of the straight line, in the limit as Δx approaches 0, is the derivative of the function f at the point $(x,f(x))$.

We can use the formal definition of the derivative to compute its value for the function $f(x) = x^2$.

We have:

$f(x) = x^2$
$f(x + \Delta x) = x^2 + 2x\Delta x + (\Delta x)^2$
$[f(x + \Delta x) - f(x)] / \Delta x = 2x + \Delta x$

The Δx term vanishes in the limit as Δx goes to 0. We are left with $2x$ as the derivative.

Table A-1 gives some derivatives of common functions.

TABLE A-1. Derivatives of common functions.

f(x)	f'(x)
ax^n	nax^{n-1}
e^{ax}	ae^{ax}
$\ln x \quad x > 0$	$1/x$
$a^x \quad a > 0$	$(\ln a)a^x$
$\log_a x \quad a > 0$	$1 / [x\ln(a)]$
$\sin ax$	$a \cos (ax)$
$\cos ax$	$-a \sin (ax)$
$\tan ax$	$a \sec (ax)$

The following rules are useful for finding derivatives of more complicated functions:

1. The derivative of a sum is the sum of the derivatives. Mathematically,
   $d[f(x) + g(x)]/dx = f'(x) + g'(x)$.
2. To find the derivative of a product of two functions: Take the first times the derivative of the second plus the second times the derivative of the first. Mathematically,
   $d[f(x)g(x)]/dx = f(x)g'(x) + g(x)f'(x)$.
3. To find the derivative of a quotient of two functions: Take the bottom times the derivative of the top minus the top times the derivative of the bottom and all over the bottom squared. Mathematically,
   $d[f(x)/g(x)]/dx = [g(x)f'(x) - f(x)g'(x)] /[g(x)]^2$

Derivatives of embedded functions are found by what is called the "chain rule." The chain rule is conceptually simple. A sample application of the chain rule is that if f changes 4 times as fast as y, and y changes 3 times as fast as x, then f changes 12 times as fast as x. This rule can be expressed mathematically as follows:

$$df/dx = (df/dy)(dy/dx)$$

As an example of the chain rule, we can calculate the derivative of $f(x) = e^{\sin x}$. Here, we set $y = \sin(x)$. We calculate the derivative as follows:

$$df/dy = e^y = e^{\sin x}$$
$$dy/dx = \cos(x)$$
$$df/dx = (\cos(x))\, e^{\sin x}$$

In a problem of Chapter 12, it was necessary to find the derivative with respect to Θ of $\cos^3(\Theta)\sin(\Theta)$. Once the derivative of $\cos^3(\Theta)$ is known, then the product rule can be used to find the final answer. But first we must invoke the chain rule to determine the derivative of $\cos^3(\Theta)$. Setting $f = \cos^3(\Theta)$, and $y = \cos(\Theta)$, we can apply the chain rule as follows:

$$df/dy = 3y^2 = 3\cos^2(\Theta)$$
$$dy/d\Theta = -\sin(\Theta)$$
$$df/d\Theta = -3\cos^2(\Theta)\sin(\Theta)$$

Now the product rule can be applied to give:

$$d[\cos^3(\Theta)\sin(\Theta)]/d\Theta = [\cos^3(\Theta)][\cos(\Theta)] +$$
$$[\sin(\Theta)][-3\cos^2(\Theta)\sin(\Theta)]$$
$$= \cos^4(\Theta) - 3\cos^2(\Theta)\sin^2(\Theta).$$

Calculation of Integrals

Following is a brief theoretical justification for using the integral to find the area under a curve.

Consider a curve f(x) as pictured in Figure B-1.

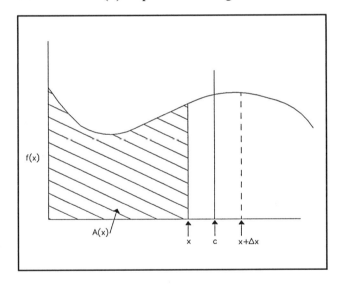

FIGURE B-1. *Deriving an equation for the area under a curve.*

Let A(x) be the area under the curve f(x) and bounded by the two coordinate axes and the value of the abscissa x. Thus, A(x) is the area of the shaded region in Figure B-1.

A(x + Δx) – A(x) is the area under the curve f(x) and bounded by the abscissa values x and x + Δx.

There is some value between x and x + Δx, call it c, where f(c) corresponds to the "average" height of f(x) in the interval between x and x + Δx. It is average in the sense that the area of the unshaded region A(x + Δx) – A(x) may be computed by f(c) Δx. (In calculus theory, the Mean Value Theorem of Areas provides a rigorous proof of the existence of the point c. In this book I am not going to prove this theorem, but will appeal to the reader's intuitive sense that the existence of c is obvious.)

$A(x + \Delta x) - A(x) = f(c)\Delta x$, by the definition of c.
$[A(x + \Delta x) - A(x)] / \Delta x = f(c)$

Now we can take the limit as Δx goes to 0. We recognize the left side as the derivative of $A(x)$. We also recognize that, as Δx approaches 0, c approaches x, since c is trapped between x and x + Δx.

Thus we have:

$dA(x)/dx = f(x)$

In words, this says that to find the area under the curve $f(x)$, we must first find the function whose derivative is $f(x)$. To find the area under $f(x)$ bounded by the two abscissa values $x = x_1$ and $x = x_2$, with $x_2 > x_1$, we must clearly take the difference $A(x_2) - A(x_1)$. In words, this means finding the function whose derivative is $f(x)$, and evaluating that function at x_2 and x_1, and then taking the difference. Table B-1 below lists integrals of some common functions.

TABLE B-1. Integrals of some common functions.

$f(x)$	$\int f(x)dx$
ax^n	$(ax^{n+1}) / (n + 1) + C$
e^{ax}	$(1/a)e^{ax} + C$
$1/x, x > 0$	$\ln x + C$
$\sin(ax)$	$-(1/a)\cos(ax) + C$
$\cos(ax)$	$(1/a)\sin(ax) + C$

In Table B-1, the constants C are necessary and represent unknowns that must be determined from further problem information. (Note: In the case of computing areas, where we calculate $A(x_2) - A(x_1)$, whatever the constant C is, it is cancelled by the subtraction, so we don't need to bother with it.) The reader can verify, for example, that the derivative of x^2 is 2x, but the derivative of $x^2 + 3$ is also 2x. Thus, when we integrate 2x and obtain x^2 as an answer, we are correct only to within an additive constant.

In Chapter 14, we claimed that the area under an exponential probability curve is 1. To show this we compute the integral:

$\int_0^\infty \lambda e^{-\lambda x}\, dx$
$= \lambda(-1/\lambda)e^{-\lambda x}\big|_0^\infty$
$= -1(0 - 1) = 1.$

Finding integrals of complex functions is more difficult than finding derivatives. Straightforward rules don't usually apply. One useful technique for integrating a product of functions is called "integration by parts." To use this technique, you must be able to integrate one of the factors of the product. The formula to use for integrating by parts is:

$\int u\, dv = u\, v - \int v\, du$

To find the mean of a random variable that is exponentially distributed, we need to take every possible value that the variable can take on, multiplied by the associated probability, and add it all up. For the case of the exponential random variable, which can take on a continuum of values, this amounts to evaluating the integral:

$\int_0^\infty \lambda x e^{-\lambda x}\, dx$

We do this using the technique of integration by parts. We set $u = x$, and $dv = \lambda e^{-\lambda x}\, dx$. Then du is just dx (since $u = x$), and we obtain v by integrating dv. Thus we obtain $v = -e^{-\lambda x}$. (In integration by parts, we don't need to add a constant at this step. If we do add a constant, we will get the same answer in the end.) Now:

$u\, v - \int v\, du = x(-e^{-\lambda x}) - \int_0^\infty -e^{-\lambda x}\, dx$
$= -xe^{-\lambda x} - (1/\lambda)e^{-\lambda x}\big|_0^\infty$

We must evaluate this expression at infinity and at 0, then take the difference. The evaluation at 0 is easily calculated as $-(1/\lambda)$, as the reader can verify.

The evaluation at infinity is tricky because of the term $-xe^{-\lambda x}$. As x goes to infinity, $e^{-\lambda x}$ goes to 0, so what is infinity times 0?

Well, it turns out that the exponential factor dominates the x-factor, and the product $xe^{-\lambda x}$ goes to 0 as x goes to infinity. If you didn't know this, you could plot the graph of the function, and verify that, indeed, the product tends to 0. But there is a quicker way.

An incredible theoretical result (which is beyond this book's scope to prove), called L'Hospital's rule can be stated as follows:

To evaluate the limit of an indeterminate form, express the form as a ratio, then evaluate the ratio of the derivatives.

In our case, we can express $xe^{-\lambda x}$ as the ratio $(x)/(e^{\lambda x})$. The ratio of derivatives is $(1)/(\lambda e^{\lambda x})$, which, as x goes to infinity, clearly goes to 0.

So the entire expression $-xe^{-\lambda x} - (1/\lambda)e^{-\lambda x}$, evaluated at infinity, gives us $0 - 0 = 0$. The expression evaluated at 0 we have previously computed as being $-(1/\lambda)$. So the difference (the evaluation at infinity minus the evaluation at 0) is $(1/\lambda)$, the mean of the exponential probability distribution.

In Chapter 14, we needed to find the probability distribution for the difference of two independent identically distributed exponential random variables. To do this, we need to evaluate a convolution integral:

$$H(z) = \int f(x)g(z + x)dx$$

Here we denote z as the random variable that is the difference of two exponentials. For the difference to equal z, the first one must equal $z + x$, and the second one must equal x. Then we integrate over the full range of values that x can have. We have:

$$f(x) = \lambda e^{-\lambda x}$$
$$g(z + x) = \lambda e^{-\lambda(z+x)}$$

The reader has the necessary tools to compute $H(z)$ as $(\lambda/2)e^{-\lambda z}$. Note that z is in the range from minus infinity to infinity. The distribution of z is sketched in Figure 14-5 of Chapter 14.

Note

Calculus and Analytic Geometry, Fourth edition, by George Thomas, (Reading, Massachusetts: Addison-Wesley Publishing Company, 1968) provided the basis for the theory of this appendix, although most calculus texts contain this theory. This book also contains a proof of L'Hospital's rule and a proof of the Mean Value Theorem of Areas.

Derivation of the Exponential Probability Distribution

Following is a simplified approach to deriving the exponential probability distribution.

Two assumptions are necessary:

1. If t represents the time since the last occurrence of an event, and h represents a small amount of time into the future, then the probability of an event occurring in the time interval (t, t + h) is independent of how big t is.

2. h is chosen small enough so that the probability of more than one event occurring within a time of size h is approximated by 0. The probability of one event in a time of size h is proportional to h. We will call this probability ah, where a is a constant.

The probability of no events occurring in a time of size t + h is: (The probability of no event in t)(The probability of no event in h) by the assumption of independence. The probability of no event in h is 1 – ah, by assumption 2 above. Denote by Q(t) the probability of no event in t. Then:

Q(t + h) = Q(t)(1 – ah) = Q(t) – ah Q(t)
Q(t + h) – Q(t) = –ah Q(t)
[Q(t + h) – Q(t)] / h = –a Q(t)

Now, we take the limit as h goes to 0. We notice that the left side is the derivative of Q(t), which we will denote by Q′(t).

Q′(t) = –a Q(t)

We have a differential equation with solution $Q(t) = Ce^{-at}$, which the reader can verify by substitution. Here C is a constant, which we must determine by more information. We can evaluate C by noting that $Q(0) = 1$, that is, in a time interval of size 0, the probability of no event occurring is 1. From this we see that, necessarily $C = 1$.

Now we have e^{-at} as the probability of no events in time t. The probability of the first event occurring before time t is then $1 - e^{-at}$. Denote by T the time of the first event. Mathematically:

$$\Pr(T <= t) = 1 - e^{-at}.$$

T is a random variable with some probability density function. The above expression is the probability that T lies between 0 and t. It is also the area under the curve of the probability density function between 0 and t. From the theory developed in Appendix B, we can take the derivative of this area function to give us ae^{-at} as the probability density function for the time until the next event. This corresponds to the exponential probability distribution of Chapter 14.

Note

A First Course in Stochastic Processes, Second edition, by Samuel Karlin and Howard M. Taylor (San Diego: Academic Press Inc., 1975), provides an excellent theoretical basis for the areas of probability and stochastic processes. It is highly recommended to the interested reader who wants to probe this subject more deeply.

Derivation of Interest Rate Formulas

In Chapter 9, we posed the question of how much money would be in your IRA at maturity. This problem represents a uniform series if all payments are of equal amounts and equally spaced. Let us imagine n payments of 1 unit each, spaced equally apart. The interest rate during each spacing will be i. After the nth deposit, how much money will be there?

Consider in turn the future worth of each deposit. The last deposit will earn no interest, so will be worth 1. The second last deposit earns a rate of interest i over one period, so will have a worth of $1(1 + i)$. Similarly, the second-to-the-last deposit will be worth $(1 + i)^2$, since it gains interest over 2 periods. The first deposit will be worth $(1 + i)^{n-1}$. We can sum all these contributions to obtain the following series:

$$M = 1 + (1 + i) + (1 + i)^2 + (1 + i)^3 + ... + (1 + i)^{n-1}$$

(Equation D-1)

We can multiply Equation D-1 by $(1 + i)$ to give us Equation D-2 below:

$$(1 + i)M = (1 + i) + (1 + i)^2 + (1 + i)^3 + ... + (1 + i)^n$$

(Equation D-2)

Now we subtract D-1 from D-2 to get:

$$iM = (1 + i)^n - 1$$
$$M = [(1 + i)^n - 1]/i$$

Also in Chapter 9, we posed the question of withdrawing from an IRA. Let us say that we start at time 0 with 1 unit. At time 1 we withdraw M, at time 2 we withdraw another M, for a total of n withdrawals, after which our original 1 unit is depleted. How big can be our value of M? We will assume as above a constant interest rate i over the length of the period.

We will approach this problem by calculating the worth of each withdrawal in terms of worth at time 0. Thus, the withdrawal of M that we make at time 1 is actually worth $M/(1 + i)$ at time 0. The withdrawal at time 2 is similarly worth $M/(1 + i)^2$ at time 0, and so forth for all the withdrawals. We can write the following series:

$$1 = M(1 + i)^{-1} + M(1 + i)^{-2} + M(1 + i)^{-3} + ... + M(1 + i)^{-n}$$
$$1/M = (1 + i)^{-1} + (1 + i)^{-2} + (1 + i)^{-3} + ... + (1 + i)^{-n}$$

(Equation D-3)

Now, as before, multiply Equation D-3 by $(1 + i)$ to give D-4 below:

$$(1 + i)/M = 1 + (1 + i)^{-1} + (1 + i)^{-2} + (1 + i)^{-3} + ... + (1 + i)^{-(n-1)}$$

(Equation D-4)

Now subtract Equation D-3 from Equation D-4:

$$i/M = 1 - (1 + i)^{-n}, \text{ or}$$

$$M = i/[1 - (1 + i)^{-n}]$$

Index